Coach's Manual:
Choreography and Style for Skaters

To the many skaters and coaches with whom I have been associated; in grateful recognition of the inspiration and confidence each gave of my work. I am nurtured by the sense that my work is valued.

Coach's Manual:
Choreography and Style for Skaters

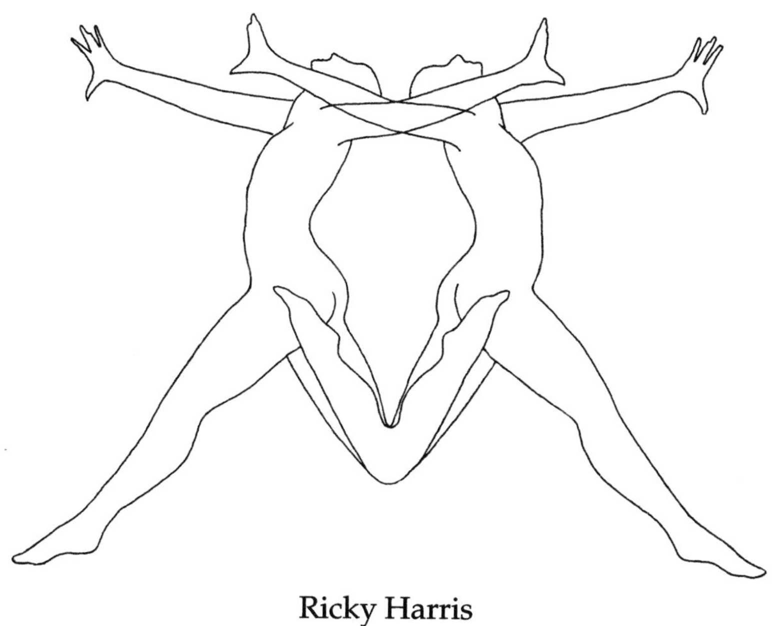

Ricky Harris

With a foreword by Frank Carroll

ISBN 1-58510-070-6

Cover design by Linda Robertson.
Cover and inside illustrations by Jerry Schwartz.
Inside photographs by Ricky Harris and Company.

This book is published by Focus Publishing/R Pullins Company, PO Box 369, Newburyport MA 01950

Printed in the United States of America
10 9 8 7 6 5 4 3 2 1

Contents

Foreword

One of my fondest memories of Ricky Harris occurred while she was creating a program for a very young Christopher Bowman. Christopher had won the bronze medal in the U.S. Novice National Championships, was not yet 12 years old, and had chosen to skate to "Birth of the Blues" for a show. We met in a ballet room [of sorts] at the Paramount Ice Rink, home to the Arctic Blades Figure Skating Club. In no time at all we were throwing ourselves everywhere...crawling on our knees, listening to the music, experimenting with all kinds of blues and sultry movements. The program was a great success, and remains one of my favorite programs of his career. The thing that is strongest in my recollection of the event was the great fun I had that day! On the drive back to Los Angeles I kept thinking how much Ricky had drawn out of Christopher; what a wonderful positive attitude she kept throughout the process of creating the piece, and finally...how much I admired her.

Ricky Harris has been a pioneer in creating a place for choreographers on ice, and in educating the public that the choreographer's place in the sport is not just to fluff arms and embellish mediocre programs. She was instrumental in establishing the Professional Skaters Association rating in choreography. She was one of the first master-rated coaches in that discipline and helped set the criteria, and much of the direction that the oral examination should take.

The list of legendary skaters she has worked with is incredible...Scott Hamilton, Michele Kwan, Linda Fratianne, Christopher Bowman, and Brian Boitano is just a few. The famous Canadian choreographer, Lori Nichol, credits Ricky with giving her the inspiration and the early basic theory of how to create and teach choreography, and often draws on these principles in her work.

In any field it is possible to acquire great knowledge, but to be able to pass on that knowledge and be a great teacher is an entirely different matter. This is where Ricky Harris excels. Her approach to teaching is organized, academic, and inspiring! She is open to all new ideas, music, movement, color, literature, etc. She is a learner, as are all great teachers!

I am so lucky to know Ricky Harris and to have her as a friend. My life is richer for it. I do wish she would disclose the location of the fountain of youth she so obviously visits.

Frank Carroll
Olympic Coach of the Year
USFSA Hall of Fame
Coaches Hall of Fame

Acknowledgements

I wish to express my appreciation to Renee Lipscomb for helping me organize my first coach's workshop. Her dedication and determination made it possible. It was through these workshops that the idea for the manual evolved. I also want to thank her and the Kennesaw, Georgia skaters for posing for photographs, although I was not able to use all of them. For the skaters in Naperville, Illinois who allowed me to photograph them—a big hug. To Candy Brown Burek, who coaches most of them, kudos for the fine technical training she gives her skaters and for dedicating herself to the education of artistic qualities at the same time. That, along with her understanding of my work, inspires me creatively. My love and thanks go to coaches Caroline Lee and Annette Thomas, who are always eager to learn and seek new information to apply to their teaching, and who took the time to be photographed. My heartfelt thanks to artist Ana Thiel, who allowed me to interrupt her busy schedule for additional photos. Thanks to Suzanne Pyle who supplied me with support and productive information. Kudos to Ron Pullins who had the courage to seek new paths; and to Melissa Massello, whose help and encouragement made this whole process a breeze.

My love and gratitude also goes to my husband, Paul Piazzese, who read and corrected the manuscript several times. His knowledge and love of the visual and performing arts afforded him the opportunity to make important suggestions that benefited the book.

Introduction

My primary motivation in life has always been the original approach. After years of experimentation, this resulted in new teaching concepts for competitive and professional skaters that helped to develop their artistic and athletic skills simultaneously.

Having been trained as both a skater and a dancer, I began teaching academic dance classes to skaters in ballet studios inside skating rinks, indoctrinating into their schedules classes in drama techniques. This culminated in workshops for skaters that I conducted internationally. I feel that skating is also an artistic endeavor; therefore, skaters should be trained as dancers and actors as well.

Composer Philip Glass, writing about changes in the music world in the latter part of the 20th century, talks about the radical ideas of John Cage that helped make those changes:

"Cage wrote eloquently (if at times obliquely) about a larger shift in the relationship between performer and listener. Music, he argued, could no longer be seen as something separate and detached from its listeners and from its context. Rather, creating music was a process that was initiated by the composer or performer, but completed by the audience. The listeners' experience of the work was essential to the music itself."

I believe the same thing can be applied to figure skating. A program should not be separate and detached from the audience but completed by them. The audience's experience of the program is essential.

I was inspired to conceive an academic approach to teaching skaters how they can develop movement styles suitable to their individual bodies and needs. This resulted in writing my first book, *Choreography and Style for Ice Skaters,* so I could reach skaters throughout the world with these techniques. I am happy to note that many competitive roller skaters are also using my book.

It is important to me that coaches become more knowledgeable about the choreographic process, in order to help their skaters develop original and individual styles. My intention in writing the music chapter was to use musical terms in ways that could be related to the choreography, knowing that many of the readers may not have a technical musical background. I borrowed the musical ideas that work well in creating a relationship between music and movement.

I recently began conducting workshops for coaches who requested written material to go along with the workshops. This inspired me to write *Coach's Manual on Choreography and Style for Skaters.*

- I -

Philosophy of Choreography

Skating should be considered a fine art. It is not simple velocity or agility that constitutes the perfection of it, but grace.

—John Adams (1781)

Skating is an art form as well as an athletic event. Art is a precious gift that enriches our lives forever and reaffirms beauty and creativity. If we become knowledgeable in the principles of art, then instruction won't simply be a matter of passing on our personal styles and idiosyncrasies to our students, but encouraging them to develop their own styles.

I believe the greatest proof of success for skating coaches who want to be choreographers is that not one of their students is remotely imitative of their style, or any two of their students' styles remotely resemble each other. To accomplish this you want to know how each skater works—their assets and liabilities—and create work that suits their abilities. As your skater matures you can help them to develop an "artistic eye" by allowing them to voice opinions about some of the choreography.

How else can we develop artistic qualities in our skaters? One way is introducing drama and expression in skater's programs, just as in the dance world. To use these tools effectively, the instrument of the body must be disciplined and prepared, so naturally I endorse training in dance in conjunction with skating.

All dance techniques have these objectives:

1. To stretch
2. To strengthen
3. To coordinate
4. To define line and form in space

A skater should be versatile and able to express any form: ballet, modern, jazz, ethnic, dramatic, and athletic. Skaters are less apt to work on expression, which dancers take for granted. This has to do with an *attitude* and wanting to express through movement what you are feeling and thinking. To choreograph effectively, all types of movement should be experienced. It is extremely valuable to know about total control of the body.

The word dance is derived from an old German root word *danson,* meaning "to stretch." It should also be the goal of all skaters to metaphorically "stretch" the audience out of their seats into space; that each person in the audience, and each judge, would be absorbed by the experience and feel like a participant, experiencing the program themselves. In essence they would be skating too.

Creative artists in any of the performing arts with the proper background and knowledge of what they want to express can more powerfully communicate the inner essence to their audience, and through empathy cause the audience to share in the experience, not merely witness the performance as a detached spectator.

Why else is dance important?

Dance training produces a responsive and coordinated body, able to perform anything the mind of the performer desires to express. When mastered, the principles of movement can be applied instantly and without conscious thought to any problem of expression or abstract movement.

We know that there is a need for more expression. What are we talking about? We are talking about turning skaters into actors. To do that, skaters must become less inhibited. Some skaters are natural actors. But when they are not, it has to be a learned process.

There is no quick way to learn this, and ideally one should start at the earliest possible age. First, one must learn to feel movement both inside and outside the body and to enjoy the way movement flows through the body, or darts from one place to another, with large amounts of energy. It is important that you learn to enjoy improvising movement, as that is where your first expression is born.

It is not good enough for skaters to skate a clean program. With so much media attention, skating has become an entertainment factor, thus making it important for programs to be performed, not just skated.

Everyone learns at a different speed, and sometimes it takes a great deal of patience to do simple improvisational exercises. Once you start to feel the movement in your body, you will begin to enjoy it and start relating movements with music.

It is most important to educate yourself in some basic knowledge of the dynamics and qualities of music. As you learn, your ears will become more finely tuned, and you will hear changes in music that can be interpreted for more expressive and exciting performance quality. All this material must be practiced and repeated consistently until the memory is built into the muscle and you don't have to deliberately think about it. It will be there.

If the coach understands these things, they can successfully impart them to their skaters. The choreography that is given to skaters by their coaches then becomes the art of the skaters, because they can feel it and can communicate it to the audience. Otherwise they are just imitating movements.

Study all the different ways a body can move. This will help to create movements that are expressive. Thinking of descriptive thoughts and making the body describe them in movement develops mini stories.

Creative people persist. If things do not come out exactly as planned, they dismiss it from their thoughts, change the idea slightly, and go on. Through persistence comes the practice that is necessary for artistic accomplishment. Creative people in all fields know that they must practice and experiment, even though they may become frustrated. They just continue. Through persistence they will achieve their goals. If they create something wonderful but no one else recognizes its wonder, they just move on and keep their minds on the future. They don't worry, because they know that worry is rehearsing for failure.

How Ballet Influences Skating

Skating has become a major theater art, so it naturally must turn to dance for ideas and patterns to follow. Both dance and skating are body arts dependent on athletic skills. Both are allied to music, especially rhythm, but each has its own strengths and limitations. A skater's movements are restricted by the slippery ice and heavy boots; yet at the same time a skater can attain greater speed and special moves impossible to a dancer.

What skaters have to learn primarily is the eloquence of expression. This begins with an attitude of the mind, resulting in an outward expression of an inner focus. This is often absent in skaters. It is something that a performer feels must be communicated. Using imagery can be important when working with emotions. If a skater is not able to relate to a particular emotion because of age or lack of experience, then it is helpful to manufacture that experience.

Space

A sense of space is equally important. It is an awareness of the variety of directions the body and its parts can take when moving though space. It is also an awareness of the intimate space surrounding the torso, head, and limbs, and how it can affect the interpretation of emotions.

Psychologically, it is a sense of the relationship between the self and space.

Body-Lines

There are four body-lines to be considered:

1. Vertical—a line that signifies power, dignity, and balance.
2. Horizontal—a line that indicates tranquility, rest, endurance and, strength.
3. Diagonal—a line that represents an energetic expression of vitality or force. There is also an indication of excitement.
4. Curved—lines that suggest warmth, loving qualities, and gentleness.

All four body-lines should be used to portray the purpose of the program. When balance is needed, vertical lines would be appropriate. When you have a skater that needs more expression in showing energy and vitality, use more diagonal lines. Use curved lines for those who need to show more warmth in their skating.

Be aware of what different body-lines suggest, especially when choreographing for inexperienced skaters. I do not imply that all body-lines cannot be used for them. I only suggest that care be taken where the different body-lines are placed in the program, so there is continuity to the theme or motivation. This applies to all skaters.

Taking Risks

To escape criticism, do nothing, say nothing, be nothing.

—Elbert Hubbard

You cannot become a great artistic skater or choreographer without taking risks. The greatest accomplishments in skating (and also in life) demand the greatest risks. History itself was shaped by the boldness, not only of collective action, but also of individual initiative.

Coaches who want to be choreographers, who panic at the thought of failure, and do not act with determination and distinctness when at a critical point, develop restrictions resulting from their fears. Fear indicates a lack of confidence. Outside classes in music, drama, or dance might spark new qualities in your work, give you new goals, and the confidence you need to take risks.

Experimentation

Experimentation is the key toward becoming a creative artist. Because skating is such a viewed art in the making, you risk criticism even before the choreography is completed by parents, other coaches, and other skaters. You can experiment with related arts in the privacy of music, dance, and art studios, but in skating, you are constantly on view by everyone. Therefore, it is important to learn to focus on your goals, blocking everything else out.

It is perfectly all right not to look "good" all the time when you are experimenting with different ways to move. The great choreographer Twyla Tharp said, *"Artists must be allowed to wallow around in their own confusion, and that can lead to other, more finished things."* You must dig around in your subconscious mind to find new thoughts and approaches that will eventually set you apart from other choreographers.

The choreographer that constantly tries to grow and experiment, and not be afraid of failure, is a highly motivated individual. Being leery of failure becomes an obstacle to development and growth. A successful choreographer must take risks. You cannot reach your goal without mistakes. Welcome the mistakes as learning processes towards fulfilling your goals. Be self-accepting, not only of your strengths but also of your weaknesses and imperfections. Then get the help you need.

Do not hesitate to be controversial. Many artists who are controversial seem to be avant-garde and in the forefront of what is happening in the world. Picasso became controversial when he developed cubism, but now it is an accepted style of expression and a part of art history. Artist Maya Lin, who won the Vietnam Veteran's Memorial design competition in Washington, D.C., was surrounded by controversy. There was a highly organized opposition to this work. Today the Vietnam Memorial is so identifiable and emotional it is difficult to believe that this could have been. At one time I was personally criticized as being controversial in my work by one of my peers. I accepted that as a great compliment, although it was not intended to be, knowing that all true creative people, at one time or another, are controversial.

Preserving an individual identity, regardless of what everyone else is doing, is difficult and challenging but highly motivating. In order not to succumb to the mundane way of doing things, there must always be experimentation and the risk of failure.

Learn to love yourself. Remember that part of maturing in your work is revealing *you*. Get involved with what is happening now. Take delight in experimenting. Explore the possibilities of yourself. You will need patience and practice to develop an awareness that grows and changes as the world changes.

> *Don't go where the path leads. Rather go where there is no path, and leave a trail.*
>
> —Old Saying, author unknown

-2-

Choreographic Ingredients

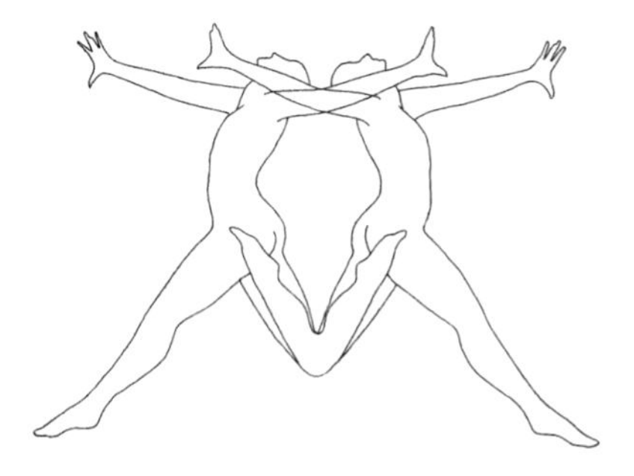

Failure to use such an abundant inherent treasure as creativity, whether it's because of unawareness that it exists, indifference or deliberate stultification; is more than a waste. It is self-betrayal.

—Masatoshi Yashimura

No two people are exactly alike, and in so far as your work expresses your unique individuality, your personality, feelings, and rhythms—it will be new. It will be creative.

Everyone is creative. Our creative imagination needs to be liberated and cultivated, and in some of us it will function more readily than in others. Therefore, let us not make the mistake of thinking that some people are creative and others are not. Rather, let us put our attention on finding ways of making creative activity available to everyone.

Improvisation

Improvisation means following your own movement feelings in the creation of forms of movement. It is important to enjoy improvisation, as that is where your first expression is born. Give yourself improvisational problems of movement covering all basic elements of force, time, space, sound, sight, and skating in relation to music, visual design, and drama. Improvising in all these areas, you will develop awareness of the expressive movement possibilities of your own body and the ability to use it in the creation of expressive movement forms.

When choreographing for a skater, try to draw out, on the highest possible aesthetic level, your skater's natural movement resources and feeling for expressive forms. There is a harmony in combining the way your skater moves naturally with technique and structure.

What about discipline? Is improvisation a kind of self-indulgence in which we allow inner feelings to flow out in a vague, undisciplined sort of way? Quite the opposite! I know of no more severe discipline than improvising on a given theme and trying to make the improvisation completely satisfying. There is no escape. It is not merely a preparation for something that is intended to be satisfying someday in the future. It must be satisfying here and now.

Technical facility grows out of systematically pursued improvisational studies. Work on themes for improvisation according to the needs of the skater. If skaters are heavy on their feet, improvise on the theme of lightness. If they are always up in the air, improvise close to the ground. If skaters' leg movements are limited, or hands inexpressive, then improvise a study using that part of the body only. If their movements are too tight, try to express feelings of looseness. If they move too slowly, explore fast movement. These are movement themes, not literary, dramatic or musical themes. Choreographers as well as skaters, like all artists, must develop craftsmanship. Craftsmanship means the ability to handle the instrument (body) and material (movement) in the creation of satisfying forms. This requires objectivity and, just as a sculptor handles chisel and stone, you must have a thorough knowledge of both. Through improvisation, the choreographer can develop craftsmanship to the point where the distinction between improvisation and composition tends to break down.

Improvisation and composition are two different kinds of experiences. Improvisation is a one-time thing, but at *any* time movements discovered in improvisation may be used in a satisfying sequence for the purpose of repetition. When this is done, it becomes a composition, a form that can be repeated. Although we spend most of our time improvising, we also compose, letting our compositions evolve out of our improvisations.

The most creative moment of a program is when it is first being created. Improvisation is a continuous process of creation, uniting content, form, and technique into an integral whole. The *content* of a program is the inner experience which the movement expresses. The *form* is the outward perceptible aspect of the experience. The *technique* is the means of perfecting the form.

The form of a program should be an organic outgrowth of the content. Content is feeling. When I use the word "feeling," I do not mean specific emotions such as fear, pain, and rage only. You can express movement feelings that cannot always be put into words. Every movement we make is accompanied by diffuse emotional states which cannot always be verbalized, but which the performer can use with awareness and control.

Like all psychological occurrences, movement feelings are only partly conscious. That is why it is a mistake to approach movement creation with too much analysis and criticism. You can up to a certain point, at the beginning, so that you can learn the basic rules of the craft of choreography. Then, as you advance, it must be experienced and not wholly intellectualized. It must be felt. Improvisation is a conscious tapping of the unconscious source of creative power.

Improvisation means being wholly involved in the creative process, deep in the aesthetic experience of movement. Aesthetic experience means joy in the expressive form of the movement for the sake of the experience itself. If you begin to create for the joy of creating—enjoying the creative experience for its own sake, rather than for some utilitarian gain—is this not the essence of art?

Choreographic Approach

You must want to enjoy choreographing and seeing results and the mechanical instrument improve. The choreographers that I admire are those who do not try to make their students over in their image and likeness. This happens when choreographers enjoy a certain look in a skater and the way they move, and try to remold those skaters they are working with in that same image and likeness, rather than give them a broad base of style.

A successful choreographer should be able to have ten skaters, give them the same training, and yet each one would have developed a personal style. When you choreograph for skaters you must create for each body and personality. You may use some of the same basic concepts, but they must be individualized. There are two ways of teaching choreography; by imitation through physical images, and by explanation. I feel it is important to be able to communicate with your skaters. You must bring out their personalities, and make their machines work well.

Training

A system of training should be applied daily to choreography, and it is up to the coach/choreographer to keep enthusiasm alive in the skater.

Training produces automatic response. Discussions with your skaters should be held as to the emotions they are to portray; which movements will get the greatest response from the audience and how important it is to train those movements. If your skaters really train the choreography in their programs, it will become a part of them when they skate. Hopefully the skaters you work with will also be in dance training. Even so, there may be times when you will have to give them special tips, such as:

Opening arms When you open your arms, you must open from the elbow first and then from the back. It's a very significant point, and one that creates a whole different illusion in the completed movement.

Turning When you turn, you must pull your body up and turn as if you were spiraling continually upward, never down.

Coordination of all is important. If the skaters can skate clean programs, they are good workers. But if they can do it with every detail correct, then they are artists. Preparation is everything and it is knowledge, because quality is a function of time, care, and commitment.

Choreographer's Tools

Basic to all choreography is the material (the skater) the choreographer has to work with:

1. Good body, well trained, or in progress.
2. Elasticity, flexibility.
3. Ability to concentrate and follow directions.
4. A "sponge"—"clay" in the choreographer's hands.
5. Know about different dance forms.
6. Trust the choreographer.
7. Don't be afraid to take risks, or to look different.
8. Carry out the ideas of the choreographer to the best of their ability.
9. Be willing to practice the choreography as much as they practice the technical elements of the program.

Let us go over each point:

Good body The skater would be dance-trained and would perform skating exercises for line, form, and strength.

Elasticity and flexability	Uses daily correct flexibility exercises.
Ability to concentrate and follow directions	Pays complete attention to every detail of what is said and shown. When a direction is given, repeats it verbally.
Be a sponge—clay in the choreographer's hands	Subjugates themselves to the situation. Soaks in all the information they can get. Does not agree or disagree. When the choreography is completed, the skaters' work—putting in their personality, charm, and talent—begins.
Know about different dance forms	If a skater has no knowledge of ballet, or how different forms of jazz moves are produced, or of the sensitivity of ethnic dance, it is difficult to skate to those kinds of music without looking like the music is just a background.
Trust the choreographer	The choreographer should be educated in knowing what is best for each body type. At the beginning, even though skaters may be shy or feel uncomfortable, eventually they won't. If they need to, they can pretend they are someone else. This is a learning process and will help them to be a more diverse and artistic skater. Sometimes skaters do not learn this until they are professional.
Don't be afraid to take risks	If skaters always want to do what everyone else does, they will never stand alone to be recognized for their own uniqueness of style. Anyone who is avant-garde is taking risks. They should not be afraid to look different.
Carry out the ideas of the choreographer	A skater may not like a move. They may think it is a weird move. But in the context of the whole piece, it may be perfect. By trying to do their best, it might become the magical move of the program. The choreographer sees the whole picture and knows what the purpose of the program is. Teach the skater to not form early conclusions and to give the program a chance to develop.
Practice	The skater should be willing to practice the choreography in the program as much as the technical elements so it doesn't get watered down. It takes additional energy to perform choreography, and skaters need to build the stamina for it.

The Performance as a Whole

The performance as a whole should be structured around two aims: unity and communication. To achieve these aims involves a great deal of organization using many different kinds of line, speed, force, and rhythm. There must also be regard for phrasing, transition, sequence, repetition, and climax. The resulting performance should produce an integrated, close-knit work of art that will have, not only variety and contrast among all its elements, but also balance and harmony.

This kind of form and structure is never a matter of spontaneous impulse on the part of the performer, though it may be designed to look that way. It is the result of careful planning that needs every ounce of intellect and, more particularly, of talent and insight the choreographer possesses. That it does not always succeed is all too common, because it can never succeed, however brilliantly conceived, without the understanding and cooperation of the performer.

In the presentation of any skating element such as a jump or spin, the preparation for the element and the transition or recession following it are of the highest importance to its successful execution, and of course to the performance as a whole. It is largely a matter of timing. Some skaters "prepare" their jumps, and all too often their spins are exhibitions of skill, isolated from the rest of the performance. It would be better to regard such special elements as resulting from a steady development to a climax, and then receding smoothly in a continuous flow.

The upper back, the chest, the eyes, and the forehead should express throughout the energy and feeling of the movement. The hands, through gesture and movement, should augment the transitions. These are dance techniques and apply equally to skating.

Coach/choreographers should give serious attention to the technique and traditions of the older art of dance. They should also be encouraged to study music as seriously as their time allows. They do not have to learn an instrument, but learning about the elements of music such as note values, qualities, and dynamics, is invaluable. In a sense, both skating and dance are but music made visible and tangible in its infinite range of meaning and expression. As a choreographer, you learn to manipulate motion to express the music. As music is the reflection of the whole experience and depth of feeling in its creator, so are the body arts of dance and skating.

-3-

Analyzing Choreography

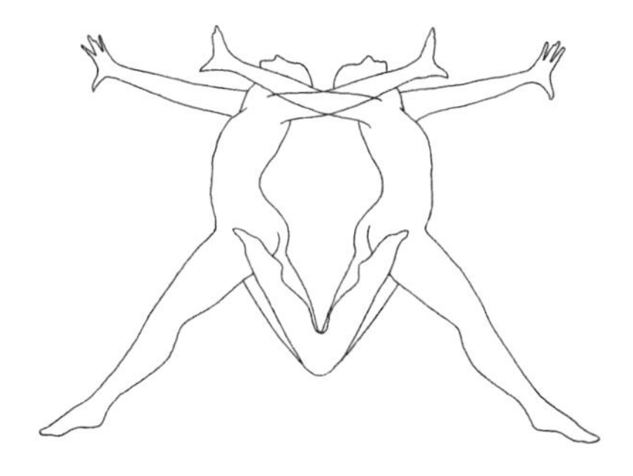

When you learn the fundamentals and "rules" of choreography, you can break them when an emotional quality demands it. It becomes a matter of feeling and understanding. It is not good when you copy someone else, so you must immerse yourself and block out everything else.

Skaters should also study choreography for several reasons:

1. They will understand movement from the choreographer's point of view.
2. They will become more familiar with choreographic terminology.
3. They will understand structure and become more efficient in their skating.

Themes

A theme is like a story line of a play. It is your subject, or it can simply be the program's face or personality. Usually, the more specific it is, the more chance you have of attaining clarity. Not all themes are suitable for skating programs.

Themes tend to fall into general categories, but it's a good idea to try a variety of them:

1. A drama or a story
2. Personal relationships
3. Basic elements of movement such as time, space, and energy
4. Pure movement themes
5. Symbolic themes
6. Characterizations
7. Tangibles and intangibles

Will the emotional content allow you to make it a skating program? If it is like a play, be careful. You must be able to carry a plot or line of development without explanation. If you need to explain it you may fail. Does each movement say what it's supposed to say at the moment? Start with one thing and everything emanates from it.

Stay away from pantomime. Pantomime is stylized realism. It is movement done in exaggeration. In acting, the actor contains his emotions. For example, if he is frightened, he is restrained and stays within bounds of realism. But the skater or dancer has a duty to express the emotional pattern within, with perhaps violent, contraction-type movements.

Contemporary skating programs should tell us something. The use of gesture can be used to show how a person feels. Certain movements can be a special visualization of an emotional pattern. In the ballet *Billy the Kid,* choreographed by Eugene Loring, double tours were a special visualization of an emotional pattern. Also, a particular gesture was used just before Billy shot someone. In the ballet *The Green Table,* choreographed by Kurt Jooss, the diplomats repeated a particular gesture to signify their group feelings. The motion and emotion of the gesture has to be made explicit, as do its cause, focus, purpose, and relationship to the program.

Intention

Intention causes the effort that creates the shape.

—Eugene Loring

The choreographer's intention can run the gamut from delighting the eye (or confusing it) to arousing memories, eliciting emotional or kinesthetic responses, and raising consciousness. It can express the joy of moving, provide surprises, or exasperate. You can have a general idea such as "Dreams" and then they can become "Nightmares." They then can be related to something else and become intensified by focusing on it.

Choreographic intention exists in both conscious and subconscious levels. That is why it so often happens that a spectator will see something in a piece that the creator hadn't planned. Possibly it was not the main intention, but part of a hidden or unrecognized one latent in the choreographer's subconscious. The spectator's discovery will also be due in part to what is brought to the piece from that person's own experiences and ideas. You as a creator can only provide the feast; you cannot control how it will be eaten, what it will taste like on different palates, or when it will be digested. What you can control is the extent in which you make the outer feelings in harmony with the inner ones. Every movement in your piece must serve that piece and that piece only. If you are true to this principle in your choreography, all the movements will be valid and will help fulfill your intention.

Skating programs need not be straight abstract works. Abstractions, mechanisms, and technology are features of our time, and, for men and women not to be robots or dolls, humor and fantasy can be retained.

Checklist

1. Is your piece abstract, or does it have a plot?
2. Does the subject allow you to be theatrical (not flamboyant)?
3. Does the subject arrest the audience and maintain interest?
4. Is there something in the beginning that makes the "curtain go up" and "come down" at the end?
5. Are there possibilities and variations of dynamics and levels?
6. Is the emotion diagrammed in space with the use of the body?
7. Do the steps belong to the central idea? Stick with the idea, and have the form follow the idea.
8. Can the audience understand the intention?
9. Is your work done in an interesting way?
10. Have you thought about what you want to say, and then think about to whom you will say it?

Choreographic Studies

A choreographic study is a short exercise in the craft of choreography that is able to stand by itself no matter what the length. There should be a beginning, middle, and end, and it could be completely abstract or be about something. It should be set so that it can be repeated the same way each time. Approach each study with the same interest and respect as you would a whole program.

The beginning is as important as the middle, and endings are not just stopping. You let the movement come to its own conclusion. You have to be sensitive to the natural phrasing and allow the movement to resolve itself. You have to love where you complete your work. Try planning your ending before you start your piece, and have the choreography melt into the ending.

I recommend looking at other choreographers' work, both on your level, and master choreographers, and observing with awareness their techniques, concepts, and the process they use. Look at lots of films and videos; go to concerts, skating competitions, and exhibitions and critique them. Learn which concepts are clear, and which are difficult to understand. Remember, there are many right answers. Look at your own work the same way. This will help in seeing the choreographic elements in other works.

Often you hear the expression "this works." What does that mean? It works when you have a feeling of satisfaction, communication of personal involvement, and a connection between the performer and the audience. Sometimes you feel that something works but you cannot express why. This comes with practice in evaluating choreography. You will eventually be able to intellectualize and verbalize why it works.

Another thing to consider in studying choregraphy is whether it fulfills the requirements that are set out, not only technically, but also the central concept of the theme you set out to accomplish. The concept must be clean and strong. Look to see if things got in the way. Ask yourself these questions when looking at yours or somebody else's work:

1. Did you meet and accomplish the central core of your assignment?
2. How did it feel? What was happening at the time that you felt that?
3. What was the unifying element, the central core of the theme?
4. What was the best moment? Why?
5. What was the high point, or climax? How was it achieved?
6. If you could make one change or suggestion, what would it be?

Watch out for having to explain your work. The movement must speak for itself. The program should have no unnecessary parts. This does not mean it has to be void of detail, but every moment tells you something. Try to get a lean, elegant statement, so the truth of your motivation can emerge. Be sure you know your intention before creating your work clearly and simply.

Before you Start

To begin an improvisation, you must be centered and uncluttered. Leave your personal problems at the door. Take 30 seconds to come to a neutral beginning. Close your eyes and focus on yourself. Let go of any other thoughts. Play with the movement. You don't have to keep the first thing that you do. You can cull your work. In skating you must learn the skill of improvising and choreographing at the same time, critically crafting and forming a program together. As your movement is flowing out, it is being shaped and developed by intuition, combined with skill into a fine organic whole. This comes with lots of practice. You can shorten the time with choreographic studies. To all this you bring an inner attitude of a commitment to create and mold and give form to skating.

Choreography is really an inner process, which begins in a creative encounter with movement and is refined with aesthetic sensibility. To achieve unity and communication involves a great deal of organized work, involving different kinds of body-line, speed, force, and rhythms. You must also consider:

1. Phrasing
2. Transitions
3. Sequence
4. Repetition
5. Climax

Ultimately you learn to choreograph by doing it, by experimenting, by creating fragments and bits of movement and movement phrases. You also learn by trying all kinds of ways to move, changing combinations around, visualizing feelings to movement, and experimenting with these kinds of movements that reproduce those feelings. There is discipline and technique to choreography. This can be learned.

All parts of choreography are related and one affects the other. However, to become aware of the whole, one must study each part, and find possibilities of combinations of these different elements.

Do not be afraid to design a skating program according to what you feel. You can combine your aesthetic feelings and your technical aptitude. You can be inspired to work to the highest standard you are capable of, exploring movement to the maximum. The important thing is to immerse yourself totally and pursue your own goals determinedly, savagely, relentlessly, on and on and on.

It is very important that the choreography be arranged so that it shows off the assets of the skater and diminishes liabilities. This involves looking at each skater as a sculptor looks at a new piece of clay. The sculptor considers the texture, color, and amount before beginning work. So must the choreographer consider the flexibility, posture, personality, music, movement experience, technical ability, and body contours before setting movement. What may look good on one skater or the choreographer's own body may look clumsy and disastrous on another. Many times movements can be created or arranged that will cover up body faults as well as technical deficiencies. I call this *corrective choreography.*

Sometimes coaches and skaters begin listening to those who are not so goal oriented, or lazy and wasteful of time. That is when you get ordinary results and your motivation weakens. The way to think is to visualize that you have on "blinders." This way you cannot see except directly in front of you, that one important road towards your goal.

A choreographer must have the proper technical background so that a creative process can always occur. Even if you get caught in a creative block, you can always go back to the fundamental tools and begin again. To choreograph, one must know oneself as well as others; one's strengths, weaknesses, relationship to the universe, potentialities, spiritual heritage, aims and purposes, and must necessarily take stock of oneself.

A choreographer should be able to guide and develop the skater into an awareness of movement, and a deeper sensitivity through which the skater can experience the various phases of life by identifying with the hopes, dreams, fears, and longings of others. Through movement the choreographer can learn to interpret these thoughts, feelings, and moods.

The choreographer/coach can teach skaters to be mentally alert to all that goes on. Teach them to be curious, observant, and imaginative, so they can build an ever-increasing fund of knowledge as a tool toward creative movement. Teach them to strive always to stretch the range of eye and ear, and take time to look, listen, and comprehend.

The choreographer approaches choreographic problems intimately, intuitively, and logically; using the light of the imagination to create, and the critical mind to judge, thereby testing inspiration with logic. A choreographer must be able to understand the structure and form of movement so that movement can be made in a more profound manner. Learning the theory of composition, along with the theory of movement, enables the choreographer, as well as the skater, to expand and find new avenues in which to experiment and discover new possibilities in which to move and express ideas.

-4-

Energy Concepts

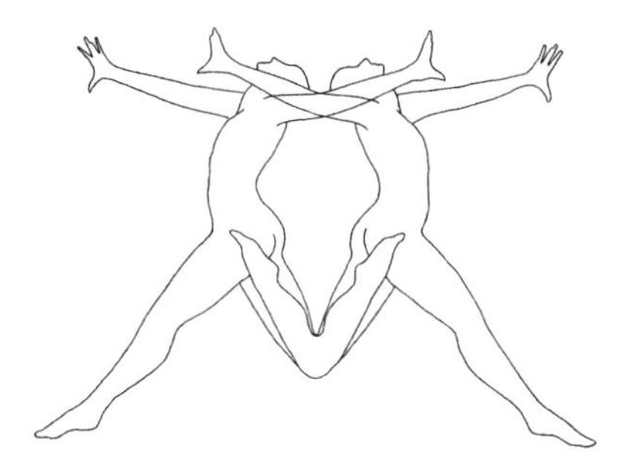

What is energy? Where does it come from? We know it comes from the sun. We all possess energy forces, not only within our bodies, but also outside in the form of currents. These currents cause a flow of magnetic energy whose supply may be constantly replenished by proper use of the existing energy around our bodies in magnetic fields. We, as human beings, have so much *potential* energy within us, that we can go through our whole lives and not use it up.

Why is it that some skaters have so little energy, while others have a great deal? It's like electric lights. Potential energy is stored there, but it only works when you flip the switch and turn it on. Thoughts create energy. Energy is power. Energy is supplied only when it is put to work. So, what is energy? *ENERGY IS A FORCE PUT TO WORK.* You can teach your skaters to tap into these energy forces and put them to work. They can then establish connections between instinctive emotional impulses and muscular reflex action, so that emotional energy can flow unblocked through a free body.

To introduce the energy concept, let us begin with a series of exercises involving improvisation. Consider that all the energy in and around the body is compressed into an imaginary energy ball that can either be in one spot of the body, or move through the body in imaginary tunnels as blood does in the arteries. Sometimes the energy ball can jump from one place to the other, causing sharp dynamics. Other times it must follow the course through the body successively to show a feeling of flow.

This energy ball concept is like magic, because I have found in all the years that I have been teaching it, most skaters at the beginning use it in a very mechanical way, focusing on the movement outside of the body. Gradually through practice, it changes to an inner focus, when the skaters begin to feel the movement and impulse coming from the inside. They become more sentient in the way they move, and the viewers see it as emotional qualities.

Single Energy Ball Flow

It is best to begin these exercises on the floor until the process is understood. Start with an imaginary ball of energy and put it inside the center of your body (midriff). Remember that the ball of energy has to be seen by the viewer, so when it is put there, a physical reaction occurs, a contraction of the center of the body. You may want to do this in front of a mirror at first, so that you can see where the ball is. Later you will want to just feel it. The entire body, except where the energy ball is, must be completely relaxed with arms hanging loosely at your sides, except when the energy ball moves them. If you have two arms up while you are working, it can be considered that you have an energy ball in each arm. Begin to move one energy ball from your center through the entire body with control. Understand that not only can you see the ball, but you can also feel it. Move the energy ball through the imaginary tunnels in succession, and go to the next closest place:

1. If it is in the center, it can go either to the chest, or one of the hips.
2. If it is in the right elbow, it can go either to the right wrist or to the right shoulder.
3. If it is in the left ankle, it can go either to the left toes, or the left knee.

These become successive movements that will create an even flow of controlled energy. *TIP: It is extremely important that the energy ball is released from where it is* before *moving it to the next place. This is how to create a flow. If this is not done, it becomes a "jumping" energy ball.*

When experimenting in moving the single energy ball around the body, make certain the ball does not "skip," but moves successively from one place to the other, e.g.:

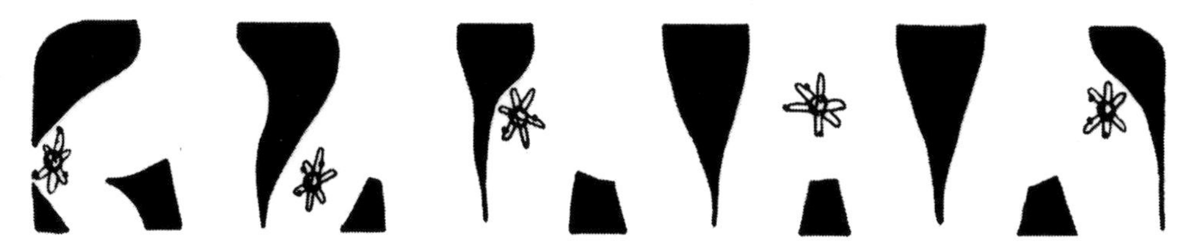

Fig. 4.1 A Path of Single Energy Balls. Feel the energy ball move from the right knee to the right thigh, to the right hip, to the stomach, to the left hip.

To move the energy ball to the right knee:

Ball moves from center....
to right hip
to right thigh
to right knee.

To move the energy ball to the left hip:

Ball moves from right knee....
to right thigh
to right hip
to center
to left hip

To move the energy ball to the fingers of your left hand, out into space, and back to your center:

Ball moves from left hip....
to center
to left ribcage
to chest
to left shoulder
to left upper arm
to left elbow
to left lower arm
to left wrist
to back of left hand
to left fingers
out into space
back into left fingers
to back of left hand
to left wrist
to left lower arm
to left elbow
to left upper arm
to left shoulder
to chest
to center

The question may arise whether the energy ball can be seen moving through the upper and lower arms and back of hands, since they are not joints, and cannot bend. The fact that you are *thinking* about it moving in those areas, helps develop inner movement feeling. A better result will be gained by doing the energy ball exercise slowly. This will give you an opportunity to feel every part of your body, and all movement possibilities.

The torso is where true emotional expression begins, and that is why it is beneficial to begin the energy ball exercises in the center of the torso. It is the most articulate part of the body besides the hands. It can hinge front, back, and side. It can rotate right and left. It can go around or do introverted actions (concave) or back (convex) or side. You can make torso circles by doing actions front, side, back and side hinges. A torso hinge is bending at the hips. Then let it spread outward, upward and downward, through the entire body. With practice, successions will display this expression through the body flow.

Criticism

When working with your skaters, help them to understand that corrections are a definite and positive approach to improvement. The process of learning anything in skating involves demonstration, imitation and then correction. As the skater progresses, there is less demonstration and more correction.

This seems to work just fine until skaters reach teenage years. Then you may begin to hear complaints such as "She is always picking on me." Or "He criticizes me constantly." The message should be loud and clear: when skaters are being corrected, they are not being criticized. Without correction, learning becomes a process of experimentation, until the right formula is found for each learned item. Every lesson will become more rewarding, and the results more definitive, if skaters listen without resentment to the corrections of their coach.

When you feel ready, try the single energy ball exercise on the ice. Experiment by using the energy ball while doing three turns, mohawks and footwork. You can teach it to your skaters, and have them constructively criticize each other, as that helps them to develop a critical and artistic "eye." Also, it teaches them to accept criticism, what they need to work on; what to do or not to do. Encourage them to experiment by using the energy ball while doing different freestyle moves. Ask them not to concentrate on trying to compose beautiful movements, but to just experiment in moving the energy ball around.

There are several "rules" to follow when working with single energy balls:

1. Use only one ball.
2. The ball must not skip.
3. Move around in space; do not stay in one place.
4. Work in different levels in space, so you are not always upright.
5. Follow the "Ricky Rule."

The Ricky Rule

Always follow the path of the energy ball with your head and eyes. This not only enables the skater to see where the ball is, but also is an automatic way of portraying expression. With constant use, an automatic response emerges. Even if you are not feeling anything, by using the Ricky Rule it will look like you are. And eventually you will feel it.

Double Energy Ball Flow

When you feel you are ready, it is time to move on to two energy balls working at the same time, flowing through the body together. Again, start on the floor in front of a mirror. It is best to use an energy ball on one side of your body, and the second one on the other side. Both energy balls move successively at the same time, but can skip to the next combination, e.g.:

1. Put one energy ball in the right shoulder and one in the left knee simultaneously.
2. Transfer one energy ball to the left elbow and one to the right ankle simultaneously.
3. Put one energy ball in the right knee and one in the left hip simultaneously.

Many different combinations can be put into use with the two energy balls, to create interesting shapes in space. This is the start of a creative process. It is more demanding than the single energy ball, but more interesting and expressive. In using the Ricky Rule, you may focus on one energy ball; then during the process, change to the other.

Again, when you feel you are ready, experiment with the double energy balls on the ice.

Jumping Energy Balls

To interpret other than slow and flowing music, it is necessary to express energy in the body in a more marked manner. This can be accomplished by allowing the energy balls to "jump" from one place to another. This is like dance isolations. Now, as many energy balls as wished can be used, and they can skip anywhere in the body. This is a lot of fun, and

Double Energy Balls

humor can be expressed by using jumping energy balls. e.g.:

Snap one energy ball
from the right hip....
to the left elbow
to right knee turned in
to left knee turned in
to both knees turned out, using two balls

A movement could start with an "impulse" which is a strong action at one part of the body, like a jumping energy ball, which could then be followed by successive movements of the flowing energy balls.

Multiple Energy Balls

Now you can begin to use as many energy balls as you wish. Let everything go and feel the energy ball in a multitude of places. At first you will feel very disorganized, but soon you will begin to relate to where each energy ball is located in your body. You will discover that you can express energy in places you didn't think was possible, opening the doors to complete expression.

Experimentation should progress along these lines, until the confidence is there to try it on the ice. When working on the floor, use music to go with the energy balls. When on the ice, listen to the music playing and try to interpret what you hear with either flowing or jumping energy balls. Accomplishment and true artistry can only come through many hours of practice.

Multiple Energy Balls

Exercises using the theory of energy in and around the body serve two purposes. They develop higher levels of energy that can be used and seen in new movements; and they also plant the seeds of improvisation, a necessary tool for the creation of movement by both the skater and the choreographer. Another benefit is the development of flow throughout the body.

By using energy balls, without realizing it you will begin to shed inhibitions. You are improvising when concentrating on the energy balls. All skaters should be able to improvise—to converse expressively through movement as easily as they converse through words, never having to stop and think of what comes next.

The ability to improvise easily and fluently is a valuable preliminary to real creation and choreography, which is deliberate in form and design, in space and time and has dynamics, rhythm and motivation Besides the physical aspects, we must recognize that thought also creates energy.

Fig 4.2: Multiple Energy Balls

-5-

Dynamics and Qualities

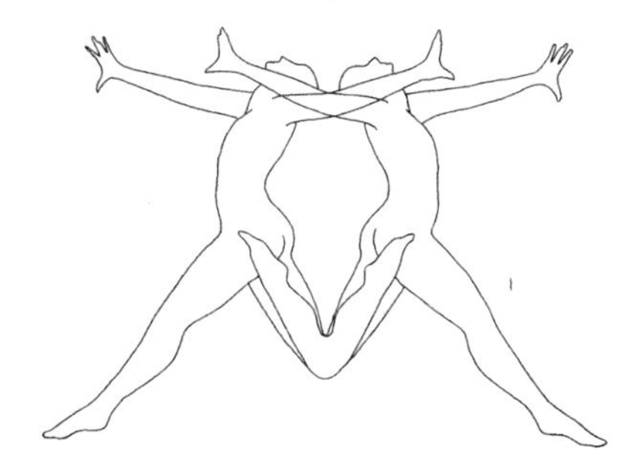

Dynamics

In music, dynamics means the amount of volume—loudness and softness. In skating, dynamics means the amount of power. Music at just one volume level would be dull. Contrast is what makes music interesting. Without contrast it becomes aural wallpaper. That is why there are different volumes of sound. This is the same in skating. It would be boring if skating programs were dynamically all on one level. Educating yourself about dynamics will help you to feel the music.

There are many gradations in the dynamics of music, but it is not necessary for you to learn all of them. Learning the meaning of just *forte* and *piano* in music, and how they can be used in movement, will make an enormous difference in the expressive qualities that you produce.

Piano in music means soft.
Forte in music means loud, or strong.

Levels Clockwise from top: High level, flight level, middle level, and low level.

Dynamics in skating is based on the effort put into movement, the amount of tension and force behind the movement. To change the dynamics from music into movement, you must think of the amount of effort you are using.

Piano

When interpreting *piano* music in movement, you would use little effort. To help grasp the idea of *piano,* imagine you are in a room filled with whipped cream. Begin improvising to soft music, and keep up a silent monologue in your mind describing how easy it is to move through whipped cream; how light your body feels, that it takes no effort to move. Use all the energy balls in your improvisation and work in different levels of space.

The high level is in an upright position with at least one foot in contact with the ice or floor.

The low level is very close to the ice.

The middle level is between high and low.

The flight level is when the body has no ice or floor contact.

Forte

Forte means loud or strong in music. In movement *forte* can be done in two ways:

Peanut Butter Forte

Imagine you are in a room completely filled with peanut butter. It would be very difficult to move your body and limbs, pushing through

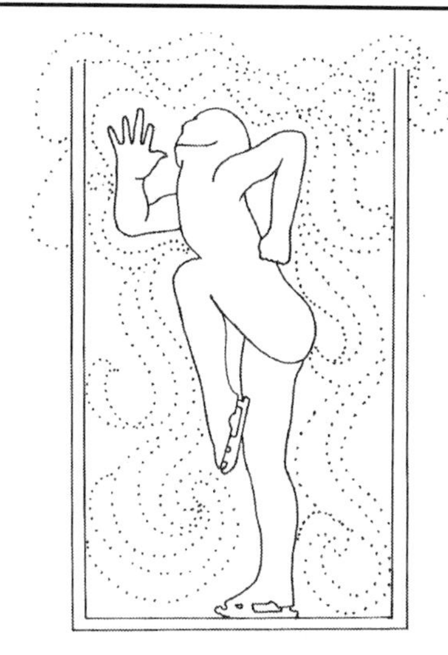

Fig. 5.1 Peanut Butter Forte
Moving with effort (*forte*) through an imaginary peanut butter mass.

this dense mass. Try to work from the inside, using your muscles to accomplish this. Place your arms in a circle in front and pretend someone has encircled their arms lightly around yours. Try to open your arms and feel that the other pair of arms is resisting your effort. You will begin to feel the quality of weight and can then practice reproducing it in other parts of your body.

The degree of muscle intensity depends upon resistance. Air has density. You can mold it, push it, or rest lightly on it as in *piano*, using little effort. By resisting air you use greater amounts of energy, and the muscle intensity is increased. When experimenting with peanut butter forte, use different levels and use the space around you. Do not forget to incorporate energy balls into the process.

Fast Forte

Fast forte is making each individual movement get to its destination with a lot of muscle intensity, quickly. It produces a forceful, fast movement. Peanut butter forte cannot be done quickly, as it is pushing through a dense mass.

The sense of weight comes from within and is guided by music and motivation. Some skaters naturally have this feeling of weight, but others can achieve it by using muscle intensity. It takes a lot of practice, and eventually it becomes an integral part of the way you move. You should be able to listen to your skater's music and identify all the dynamics, then transfer them to movements in their program. Taking a movement and doing it in *piano*, then changing it into peanut butter forte does not change the design, just the dynamic, and it creates an entirely different emotion. Even though you are using the same movements, it will look different. You can do the same by turning piano movements into fast forte and it will look like new movement. This is a tool to get variety, but in essence, it is repetition

Exercises for piano and forte

1. Improvise 16 counts of *piano*. Put it into a composition.
2. When completed and repeatable, perform the exact composition in

peanut butter forte.

3. Improvise another 16 counts of *piano* completely different from the first one.
4. After it becomes a composition, repeat it in fast forte.

   Use energy balls.

   Use levels.

   Use the space around you.

   Use the Ricky Rule.

You will find that the piano and fast forte pieces, although using the same movements, will look completely different from each other. This is a good tool to use when a piece of music is repeated with different intensity. It also adds interest to the choreography.

Qualities

In the structure of music, we also find analogies to other musical concepts. Using just three qualities in music can guide you tremendously toward the type of movement that will express the music.

Legato

In a musical score you can identify legato if you see two notes with a curve above them, attaching them together. They are notes that are connected together. These notes are tied together without a pause. You cannot hear where the music actually begins or where it ends. It is like a slur. When a phrase comes to an end, another one is coming in without a pause. "The Impossible Dream" from the musical *Man of La Mancha* is an example of a song in legato.

To transfer this concept into movement, it means that all your movements are connected together when moving to legato. You would not see a definite beginning or ending of any move. Just at the end of one movement, another begins.

Some examples in skating that would be considered legato are edges, spirals, spins, Ina Bauers and spread eagles. A series of arm movements without a stop anywhere would be Legato. *When practicing the theories encompassed in this book, try to incorporate all you have learned previously.*

Exercises for legato

1. Improvise a legato work, not less than 16 counts.
2. Use energy balls and dynamics.
3. Do part of it in piano and part in peanut butter forte.
4. Use levels and space.

Marcato

Marcato

Marcato notes in music are long notes that are clearly defined and marked. They have a definite beginning and end. The beats are separated, marked and steady; like going up a musical scale. It has a march-like quality to it. Tango music is usually in marcato. Another example is the song from *The Sound of Music* that begins: "Doe, a deer, a female deer." "The Jets Song" from *West Side Story* also uses marcato articulations. Transferring marcato into movement would mean movements that are long, and where you can see the beginning and end of each move.

Some examples in skating are split jumps, kicks and jump landings.

Exercises for marcato

1. Move an arm from the shoulder joint anywhere in space to a stop, keeping elbows and wrists straight.
2. Kick out straight with one leg as both arms go straight up.
3. Bend your torso over from the hip joints as both arms go straight out.
4. Experiment with marcato movements in piano.
5. Experiment with marcato movements in forte.
6. Incorporate levels in your work.
7. Use space and the Ricky Rule.

Staccato

Staccato in music has a sharp attack to each note. You can hear the beginning and end of each note as in marcato, except that each note has a shorter sound. An example in music is Beethoven's *Fifth Symphony*. Each note is separated and played with an attack that is touched and quickly taken away. It is like a quick action separated in time from the next.

Staccato is like touching a hot stove and quickly removing your hand. If you did a marcato movement with your arm, you would move your entire arm from your shoulder joint. If you used your arm for staccato, it may encompass two or three movements; one from your shoulder, one from your elbow, and one from your wrist.

Moving to staccato can be very humorous, and fun to use in a program. I used a staccato piece from the ballet *Sylvia* by Delibes for Scott Hamilton. We called it his "futzy part." Scott had a flair for comedy, and this suited him perfectly as he performed it with a straight face. He used it for the first time in a competition in England and it was a huge success. I believe it was the first time comedy had been choreographed into a competitive program.

Exercises for staccato

1. Use the smaller joints of the body to move, e.g. the wrist, the ankle, the elbow, as well as the knees, the head, and the ribcage.

2. Experiment with several energy balls at a time. Think of how many different ways these joints can move in space.

3. Work with levels and The Ricky Rule.

4. Do staccato in both piano and forte.

Music should not be used as just a background, but interpreted throughout so there is a sureness in time to the music. A basic knowledge of dynamics and qualities in music would certainly help upgrade the second mark of the free skating program.

Experimenting with musical qualities and dynamics, and transferring them to movements, will help you to develop an expressive style as you explore these new relationships with movement. It will add new dimensions to your choreography.

-6-

Elements of Movement

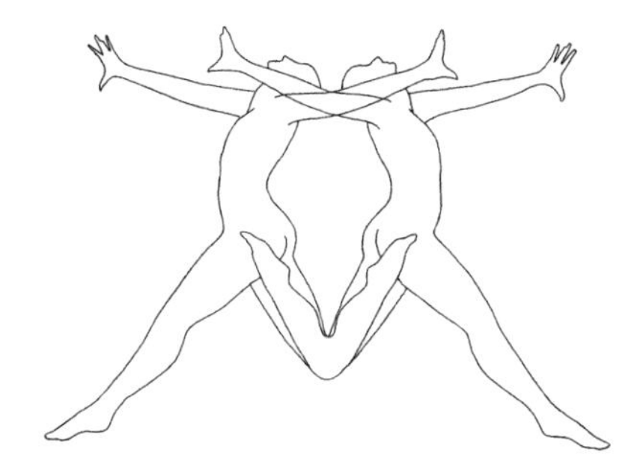

The reason we study elements of movement is for:

1. Variety
2. Expression
3. As an accent
4. An aid to balance
5. Interest

The following is a list of elements of movement that we all experience in some form throughout our lives. Taking these elements and using them for the purpose of choreography is a tool that can often solve a choreographic problem. Experimenting and improvising using these elements will provide a multitude of material that can be used in creating just the right move for a particular place in your choreography.

When working with these elements, use all the different parts of the body to perform them. Stay away from the literal meaning of the word and think of another part of the body to experiment with the element. What you will be doing is abstracting the element into an artistic and interesting move.

Element	**Physical Description**
Ascending	Moving up with control
Descending	Moving down with control
Falling	Once begun, no control—succumbing
Extending	From a bend to a straight—unfolding
Bending	Arc—from a straight to a bend
Leaping	Jump—out in space, taking up distance
Turning	Move—from one direction to another
Darting	Like an arrow—shooting out to a target suddenly into space
Hopping	Small, bouncy jumps or leaping on one foot
Swinging	Swaying movement between two points that is anchored
Skipping	Hopping-type movement that alternates between two parts
Running	Alternating parts in a forward direction very quickly
Twisting	Turning against a base in an opposite direction.
Rolling	A circular movement in space.
Shaking	Moving two parts simultaneously in very small staccato movements (quickly)—can do with one part at times.
Pushing	Using a part of the body in a forte way to move an imaginary substance.
Bouncing	A hopping procedure without moving off a base.
Pulling	Opposite of pushing—bringing something towards you in forte—an extension to a bend.
Kicking	Quick, staccato, dart-like movements against a real or imaginary object.

Tapping	Using the top of a part or an isolated part of a whole to touch quickly and lightly in pizzicato (quicker than staccato).
Striking	Can be done with one or more parts of the body, usually with an extension
Floating	Moving in space without moving parts.
Jerking	Small contorted staccato movements.
Walking	Moving parts in a progressive manner, not extended.
Sliding or Gliding	Smoothly flowing in one level—no ups or downs. Examples of slides: 1. Knees apart and in 2. Body together and slide apart 3. Slide on heels 4. Slide on wrists 5. Bashful slide with foot 6. Curl body on floor and slide 7. Knee slides
Jumping	Hips go up—height to be achieved. Examples of jumps: 1. 2 feet to 2 feet 2. 2 feet to 1 foot 3. 1 foot to 2 feet 4. 1 foot to same foot 5. 1 foot to opposite foot

Exercises for elements of movement

1. Do a choreographic study using each element of movement on the list, with a minimum of 16 counts.
2. Use a variety of different parts of your body.
3. Choreograph the study so that it moves in space.
4. Remember to include everything you have learned so far: energy balls, dynamics, and qualities.
5. When you have completed the above, experiment with combinations of elements, at least three at a time:
   1. Shaking, Bending, Pushing
   2. Extending, Twisting, Turning
   3. Bouncing, Ascending, Rolling

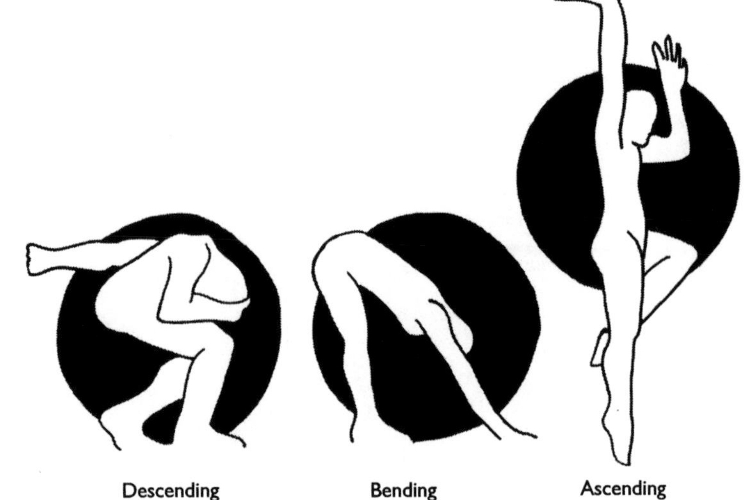

Fig. 6.1 Elements of Movement

4. Running, Swinging, Skipping
5. Shaking, Darting, Rolling
6. Gliding, Pushing, Turning
7. Bouncing, Crawling, Twisting
8. Falling, Pulling, Bending
9. Descending, Swinging, Extending
10. Crawling, Kicking, Gliding
11. Bending, Swinging, Skipping
12. Hopping, Skipping, Pushing
13. Shaking, Pushing, Falling
14. Kicking, Extending, Ascending
15. Ascending, Darting, Rolling
16. Turning, Twisting, Pulling
17. Leaping, Swinging, Descending
18. Hopping, Shaking, Kicking
19. Rolling, Pulling, Bending
20. Bouncing, Falling, Jumping
21. Extending, Darting, Twisting

Pushing Pulling Twisting

22. Turning, Running, Crawling
23. Skipping, Pushing, Ascending
24. Running, Descending, Gliding
25. Leaping, Extending, Kicking
26. Falling, Pulling, Bending
27. Bouncing, Gliding, Crawling
28. Turning, Pushing, Darting
29. Shaking, Tapping, Rolling
30. Hopping, Twisting, Skipping
31. Darting, Tapping, Hopping
32. Swinging, Descending, Extending
33. Skipping, Twisting, Shaking
34. Bending, Turning, Jumping
35. Rolling, Pushing, Bouncing
36. Descending, Ascending, Extending
37. Hopping, Skipping, Running
38. Descending, Tapping, Extending
39. Falling, Bending, Gliding

40. Pushing, Crawling, Bouncing
41. Pulling, Kicking, Leaping
42. Ascending, Falling, Gliding
43. Kicking, Swinging, Falling
44. Turning, Darting, Jumping
45. Twisting, Rolling, Shaking

Remember, you are not doing these literally. Use all the different parts of your body to accomplish these combinations. Try to use transitions in between the elements.

Additional advanced elements

1. Bumping
2. Crowding
3. Disintegrating
4. Evolving
5. Exploding
6. Flying
7. Pulsating
8. Shrinking
9. Spinning
10. Starting and Stopping
11. Tilting
12. Tumbling
13. Undulating
14. Vibrating
15. Withering

The Choreographic Process

You are now ready to proceed with *Choreographic Studies*.

1. Have a beginning, middle, and an end.
2. Have a theme.
3. Set it clearly so that it is repeatable.

(Review *Choreographic Studies* in Chapter 3.)

Thoughts Before you Start

Be flexible. You can start to choreograph a certain way, with a particular theme or thought. You have the choice of saying, "I must stick to my original idea and make it work," or realize that something else is happening and put the original idea on hold and explore a new direction. Sometimes choreographers order movement one way, only to find out that it works better another way. At all times there should be a reaching out and exploring in order to incorporate any imaginative means for an expansive presentation.

Think of music as form moving in sounds. It is the music that wants you to do certain things. Skating should look like music. If you use music simply as an accompaniment, then you don't hear it. Let your emotions in your subconscious translate into movement.

Endings

Make endings dramatic and confident. It is the finish, the conclusion of the entire skater's efforts, and it says: "There, I did my best." This is the opportunity for choreographers to show faith in their work and for what they can do in the future. The ending should be positive and full of hope. It can be simple but expressive or difficult and exciting. Many times it is fun to choreograph the ending before the beginning. You then have a goal toward which to work. This sometimes eases the choreographic process when you are not sure of how to proceed, and sets a style to work with.

Avant-garde skaters in the past have broken the ground and paved the way for interesting, innovative, and exciting movements. You can do anything without worrying about whether it will be accepted. After all, it is the end, the finish, and your skater has skated all the necessary elements for technical points. Now the ending should add to the artistic quality of the program, upgrading the presentation points.

What you design has much to do with how many counts of music are left to complete the ending, as well as what style and feeling you are trying to project. Listen to the music carefully and find the exact amount of counts that you have. Determine whether they are evenly counted or the rhythm is broken up into syncopation. You may have an even count of 1 2 3 4, or a syncopated rhythm of 1 & uh 2 & uh 3 4. Clap these counts by clapping louder on the stressed digits. Once you have your exact counts, you will have a better idea of how many moves you need to make. If you have already choreographed the whole program, you will have a fairly good idea of the music and the movement style it develops. This should show in the ending.

You can choreograph the ending by playing the music over and over and improvising until you hit on something that feels good and looks good. Or, you can deliberately design the moves methodically. One thing to think about, no matter how you design your ending, is balance. Remember, the skater has just finished the program and may be tired. Skaters should be able to hold their ending position for three counts before taking their bows.

Make the ending something important. Make a statement. Make the judges and the audience remember your skaters. After all, it is the last picture they will see of them.

1. Be sensitive to natural phrasing.
2. Allow movements to resolve, come to a close.
3. Don't be rushed. Obey your internal timer.
4. Use transitions in each study.

Transitions

A transition is an action that follows a move that leads into another move. It is something that connects two moves together. In presenting a spin or a jump, ultimately what you are striving for is the transition, or something following the element that is exciting and interesting, that will lead into the next element.

Create the choreography so the skater is "dancing" in and out of the elements. Many skaters "prepare" their jumps. At the beginning, young skaters sometimes have to do that. But as soon as possible you want them to use transitions.

Exercise for transitions

1. Experiment with transitions before and after all jumps and spins.
2. Include everything that has been discussed so far:
   a. Energy balls
   b. Dynamics
   c. Qualities
   d. Elements of Movement
   e. Use of Ice or Floor
   f. Levels
   g. Ricky Rule

Transitions bring out the artistry in the skater. They are all the things the skater does between the jump and spin elements. They tell a story. They communicate with the audience. Transitions play a very important part in the second mark in competitions.

-7-

Focus

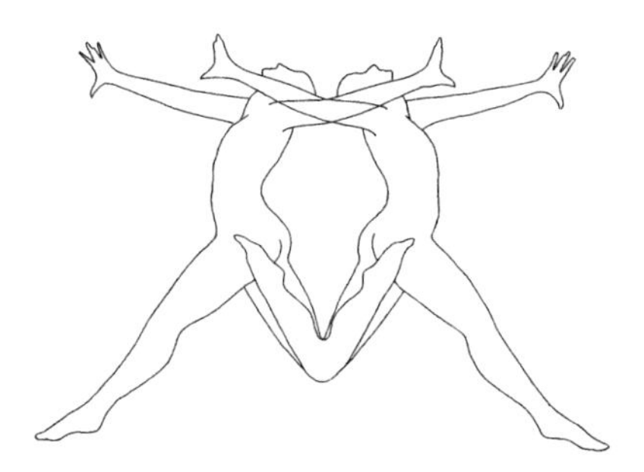

Focus is a center of awareness and attraction, when things come to a point. It is to concentrate on a thought, idea, or emotion. It results in accomplishment with strength. The awareness of the different dimensions of focusing can enable the choreographer to become more proficient and dramatic.

Many of these focus exercises can be used as tools in the choreographic process to create different kinds of movement that would be unique to each body.

Directional Focus

Directional focus takes you places. It is the placement of the head. Every coach has their own technique of teaching, but the choreographer needs to be aware of the placement of the head for artistic purposes:

1. While stroking
2. Before and after spins

3. Before and after jumps
4. During artistic moves

A knowledge of the directions of extension in ballet exercises can provide a guide for the placement of the head when using ballet arms. Many elite skaters know that placing your head slightly to the right can help stop the rotation of a jump landing.

A direction that is repeated quite often by coaches is "keep your head up." In small children this can sometimes cause bad habits. Lifting the head gives the illusion of greater height and gives more stretch to the body, but the lift should come from the back of the neck. The chin should not be lifted, and there should be no creases in the back of the neck. It is much better to educate the skater in the many different directions of head focus, resulting in various dramatic nuances that can create interest in the program.

The head can be blank as if it were unattached to the body, or it can follow the movement (Ricky Rule). Caution your skaters to use their eyes to see and to look, not just to stare. Artistically, you cannot use body forms without using the head, face, and eyes.

There are 17 head focus points:

1. Up
2. Down
3. Side Left
4. Side Right
5. Tilt Left
6. Tilt Right
7. Diagonal Up Left
8. Diagonal Up Right
9. Diagonal Down Left
10. Diagonal Down Right
11. Under Curve Left to Right
12. Under Curve Right to Left
13. Over Curve Left to Right
14. Over Curve Right to Left
15. Full Circle Left to Right
16. Full Circle Right to Left
17. Straight Ahead

When choreographing a program, insert as many head focuses as possible into the choreography.

Narrow Focus

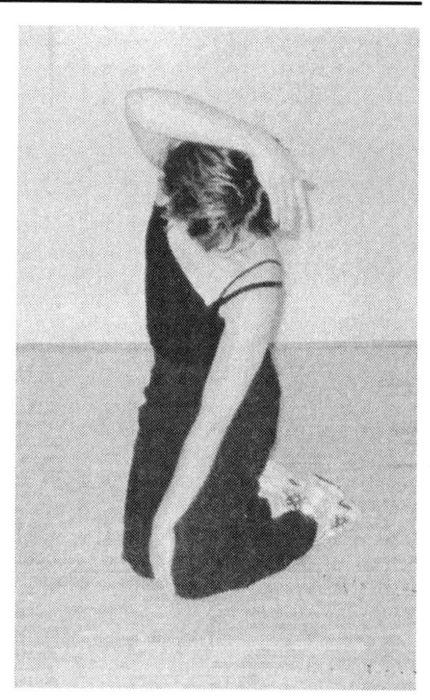

Floor Focus

Area Focus

This is a specific feeling of the amount of space around you. When working with specific amounts of space you will tend to produce movement that complements that space. Remember, these are tools only to create different kinds of movements. A good way to do this is to find music that gives you the spatial feeling you want, and then improvise to it, keeping the idea in mind of moving only in that space.

1. **Narrow or Solitude**—small space. It might help to think of yourself encased in an empty giant paper towel tube. What kind of movements can be done in that narrow space? You cannot do extended movements. They must be ones that are close to the body. Experiment with levels within that space. Think of the different elements of movement you might be able to create in that narrow space.

2. **Ice or Floor Surface**—In this category your eyes must never leave the ice or floor, no matter what kind of movements you are improvising. You will find a very emotional and dramatic feeling will be aroused. Experiment with all that has come before this, and especially the two fortes.

3. **Walls and Ceiling**—Now you will be relieved to focus on something other than the floor. Your choreography will change as you improvise and you will feel a sense of relief.

Walls and Ceiling Focus

Infinity Focus

4. **Area of Horizon or Infinity**—Pretend you can break through the walls, across the ocean, into space. Improvise with a feeling of abandonment and freedom. You will find you are improvising more leaps and jumps.

Exercise for area focus

Choreograph studies for each four of the phases of area focus. Find some music that gives you that feeling. It does not have to be cut. Think of all the things you have done before this and include them in your studies.

Dynamic Focus

This is using two contrasting dynamics or emotions with various gradations. It is an internal intensity in time and space. They could be sudden or change gradually. This type of contrast can put more character into a program. Of course, everything depends on the music and the skater.

Examples of contrasting dynamics:

1. Unafraid/Fear
2. Nervous/Confident
3. Advance/Retreat
4. Aggressive/Mild
5. Hesitant/Bold
6. Exuberance/Despair
7. Victorious/Defeated
8. Slow/Fast

9. Strong/Weak
10. Quiet Joy/Intense Joy
11. Quiet Anger/Intense Anger
12. High/Low
13. Legato/Marcato
14. Friendly/Unfriendly
15. Angry/Happy
16. Clumsy/Graceful
17. Happy/Sad
18. Introverted/Extroverted
19. Sleepy/Awake
20. Excited/Bored
21. Confused/Understanding
22. Hot/Cold
23. Strange/Normal
24. Pretty/Ugly

Doing a choreographic study to any of the above contrasting dynamics will stir up many emotions, and through movement, you will be able to portray these emotions.

Body Focus

This is an awareness of the way different parts of the body can move in space. It gives color and contrast to your work. We discussed previously how you could use any part of your body to move with the different elements, qualities, and dynamics. Even when there is only one tiny part of the body moving, the rest of the body serves as a background for that part, and so is active in a visual way. By focusing on the part as distinct, its unique capabilities and limitations become more apparent.

When considering body parts, don't forget the face, which is often neglected in skating, and sometimes becomes a starched expression of a highly expressive instrument. The face has a limitless capacity for expression, so take care to emphasize it, as well as the eyes, mouth, jaw, neck, and cheeks.

Exercises for body focus

1. First, write your name in the air with your finger, exaggerating every movement so all the letters become very large. You might have to jump to cross a "t," and bend very low for long letters.

2. Experiment with different parts of your body writing the different letters, using as much space as you can.

3. With the list below, create choreographic studies using a different letter in your name. Be sure everything is very extended and exaggerated.

a. Shoulder	b. Head	c. Wrist
d. Nose	e. Chest	f. Waist
g. Hip	h. Knee	i. Ankle

j. Foot—touching the floor in different ways:
   (1) Ball of foot only
   (2) Heel only
   (3) Alternately with heel and ball

You will find some unique movements arising from this exercise. Your body will work in ways you might not have thought of before. Use this as another tool.

Arm Focus

The arms can produce patterns in space by thinking of them as paintbrushes. Start with the basic designs of circles, squares, lines, and triangles. The arms can draw these geometric designs, or parts of them, in the space around the body while stroking, spinning, or between jumps and spins. Taking parts of these basic designs and connecting them in different ways to each other to form an interesting movement can derive unlimited gestures.

Each movement of the arms should have a connection to an inner feeling. Making a gesture just to fill a space leaves something more to be desired. It is not completely satisfying. Even when a choreographer sets an arm for the skater, there should be a motivating thought that produces that particular gesture. It is then the responsibility of the choreographer to discuss the motivation with the skater so that the gesture becomes truly the result of the thought.

Through improvisation, many arm gestures can evolve. Keep in mind that there is always the danger of a gesture looking mechanical and meaningless when performed while the skater is concentrating on a difficult element still to come. When this happens, it shows in the language of the body, the head, and the eyes. To make gestures a truly artistic product, they have to be deliberately rehearsed, perfected, and connected to an emotional feeling at a particular point in the program.

Arm movements that have a tendency to look a little weak can be strengthened by moving a different part of the body in opposition to it, such as head or shoulder. Doing a different movement with each arm will express more force and power. When opposite arm movements are combined with successive movements, it adds strength to the successive movement. (See Chapter 11.)

When movements flow through the arms and finish below the hips, they take on a more physical and sensual character. When they end in the space around the upper torso, they look pure and strong morally, emotionally and spiritually. If, on the other hand, movements end behind the body, there is a negative indication of perhaps fear or rejection.

Hand Focus

Hands can be everything or nothing to a skater. They fill the space around the body. They help the arms in balance. They create the atmosphere with a gesture and give direction to movement. Hands change with every style of movement, and in many dance forms the hands are the dancers.

Mudras are traditional classic East Indian hand gestures. There are 57,000 catalogued positions. The dancers tell stories with their hands, and accompany these mudras with body and feet movements. If you know the meaning of some of these hand gestures, it is interesting and fun to interject them into your choreography.

Exercises for hand focus

1. Put your palms together in front of your chest. Without releasing your palms, move your arms in every direction possible, allowing shoulders and elbows to stretch and bend as necessary.

2. Fix wrists together; let your fingers move as much as possible.

3. Separate hands. Make fists. At first straighten arms, then bring fists close to your body, then away; opening and closing fists.

   (A limp wrist on a man looks effeminate. Limp wrists on a woman denote weakness).

4. Experiment with the following expressive hand gestures:

a. Palms down	Blesses
b. Palms forward	Rejects
c. Palms verticle	Divides
d. Palms clutching	Greed, possessiveness
e. Palms out to sides	Giving, receiving
f. Fist	Threatens

Hands next to the face are capable of infinite meaning and expression. Experiment with movements of the hands in different areas in space, top of the head, back of the head, forehead, and cheeks. The emotional quality will change depending on the location of the hands.

Face Focus

There are always some skaters who naturally know how to project, but they are in the minority. Having a coach say, just before their skater steps on the ice to compete, "Don't forget to smile," may result in artificiality, or, when they get to a difficult part in their program, a blank stare. They may then be labeled as having a lack of showmanship.

Many skaters have wonderful technique, but they lack expressiveness. As a choreographer, it is advisable to help your skaters develop the qualities that define showmanship. This is the connection between themselves and the audience. Giving them exercises to help develop a spark that creates an invisible thread between the audience and themselves will ultimately aid in gaining higher points in the second mark. One way is by practicing face focus.

Exercises for face focus

1. Stand or sit in front of a mirror. Begin by making funny faces using all the muscles of the face.
2. Laugh and frown at your mirror image
3. Knit your eyebrows together, then release them
4. Practice raising one eyebrow at a time.
5. Narrow your eyes until they are slits, then open them as wide as possible.
   a. Open them while raising your eyebrows.
   b. Open them without raising your eyebrows.
6. Practice all kinds of smiles:
   a. Big smile, showing all your teeth.
   b. Big smile, showing no teeth.
   c. Big open smile with teeth apart.

Skaters should skate from the top of their heads to the tips of their toes including their faces. If they enjoy skating, they should show it. Feeling it inside is not enough. They must give it out freely. Becoming very familiar with one's own face in detail is essential to the eventual control of facial expression. Practicing expressions consistently will help develop a look of radiance and eventually it will become natural and a part of the skater's individuality and personality.

-8-

Design in Space, Ice Surface, and Time

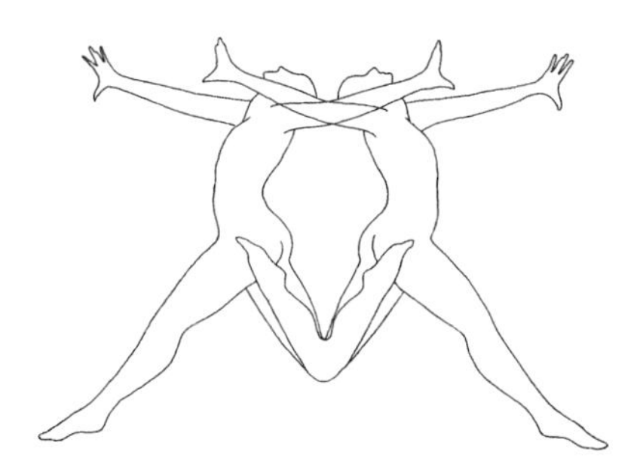

Space bends. Motion is relative. Motion and rest are relative to each other; therefore time is relative to motion.

These are the theories that Albert Einstein brought to the scientific world that imbued not only science, but also all the arts, with new creative thinking.

In the arts of painting or sculpture, you can study the designs of both as long as you wish, as they are still. Understanding movement designs, however, demands more concentration than any of the other visual arts because movement designs have mobility. They are transient rather than graphic. When the audience leaves, what it takes with them is a phantom-like thing—something thought of, made, and performed that has vanished, living on in their memory.

The human body in space can be moving sculpture, a real or abstract painting, or a poetic and aesthetic experience. It can be a form of communication, just as in drama or music. Compare the choreographic structure in skating to the structure of literature:

Language	Skating
Word	A body or tracing design.
Phrase	Phrase pattern (more than one body or tracing design).
Sentence	Phrase group (more than one phrase pattern).
Paragraph	A program section.
Chapter	A fast or slow part.
Book	The complete program.

Every movement of your head and torso, as well as the way you place your hands and legs in space, causes changes in the shape of your body. Each change is a design in space. All designs are based on geometric figures. Using these figures as an inspiration for forming designs in space is another way to invent movement. You can use a shape literally, graphing it in the space around your body, or you can create a design that is the essence of the shape.

Use six geometric figures that can be used in a literal way, or as an essence thereof. There are two ways these designs work in space:

1. Through body designs.
2. Through tracing designs.

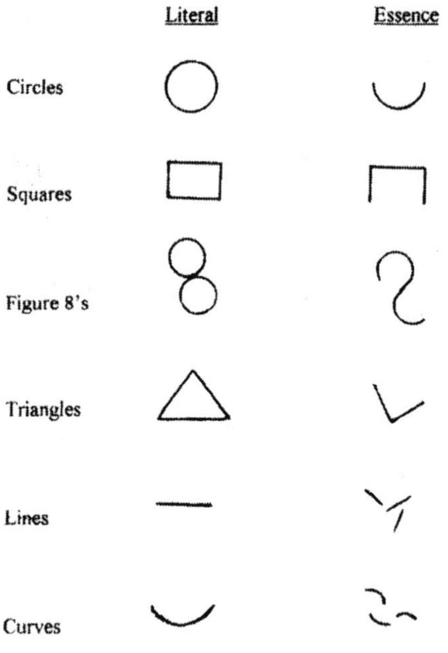

Fig. 8.1 Geometric Shapes in Space

Body Designs

Using your body and limbs to form a shape in space is called a body design. For example, when your arms form a circle above your head it makes a visual shape that can be seen as long as the position is held. It is like a photo. The design remains the same for the length of time that it is held.

Circle body designs

Exercise for body design

1. Create two examples of each of the six geometric figures in body design. One should be literal, and the other in essence.
2. Use arms, legs, as well as torso to form the design. A lot of experimentation is necessary to find the right design to match the figure. Use different parts of the body for the literal and essence.

Triangle body design

Square body designs

Figure 8.2 Figure 8 and square tracing designs

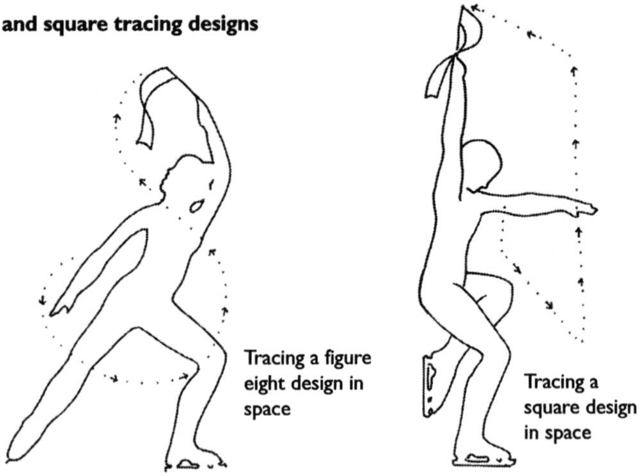

Tracing a figure eight design in space

Tracing a square design in space

Tracing Designs

These are designs that are drawn in space with your limbs and other parts of your body. It is like using a paintbrush and painting on air. You cannot see the whole picture at once as you do when making a body design, as it passes through time until it is finished; but it can be remembered when completed.

A good way to experiment with tracing designs is to practice making them with body focus, which calls attention to shapes made by the way different parts of the body move. (See Chapter 7.)

Body Focus List

Elbow	Head	Arm(s) Hand(s)
Hip	Shoulder	Knee(s)
Foot	Ribcage	Nose

Exercises for tracing designs

1. Trace a design in the air using one part of your body at a time using the geometric figures. Select from the Body Focus List.
2. Draw them literally.
3. Draw them as the essence of the figure.
4. Include dynamics, qualities, elements of movement, levels, and space.

Phrase Patterns

A phrase pattern is two or more designs in succession that are related to each other, e.g.:

Phrase Pattern I

Stroke into a forward attitude position, mohawk, back attitude (using a tracing design), axel, land; go into an attitude using body and tracing designs.

Phrase Pattern II

Do a series of different spirals in various directions. Use different body and tracing designs.

Phrase Pattern III

Do an outside to an inside spread eagle followed by an Ina Bauer, with body and tracing designs.

Exercise for phrase patterns

Create your own phrase pattern of several different but related designs. When interpreting musical phrases into movement phrases, ordinarily the music and the movement phrase would begin together and end at the same time. When this is not done, one could say the skater is skating "out of phrase." An example of this would be when a musical phrase ends in the middle of a spin and a new phrase begins before the spin is completed. The spin might have retained the same quality and dynamics throughout, but the new musical phrase may have a different quality and dynamic. Sometimes, because of the way the music is cut, you will find yourself in this position. You can put the spin somewhere else in the program where it will better suit the music, or when the new phrase begins, create a definite change in the form and dynamics of the spin that will reflect the new musical phrase.

Phrase Groups

A phrase group is like a sentence. It makes an independent statement. It completes a purpose. Adding one or more phrase patterns to those listed above will make them into phrase groups, e.g.:

Phrase Group I

Add to Phrase Pattern I (above) a step forward on the left foot, an inside 3 of the right foot; and right into a flying camel combination spin with several changes of body designs including attitude positions. What you added is another phrase pattern. The two phrase patterns together now form a phrase group.

Phrase Group II

Add to Phrase Pattern II (above) a series of inside 3's on a right inside edge, with the left foot in a low attitude position. Add an interesting stop. These two phrase patterns now become a phrase group.

Phrase Group III

Add to Phrase Pattern III (above) two back dutch rolls to a double lutz. This now becomes phrase group III.

You can close your eyes and picture different movements in your head and connect them together until a phrase picture forms. Sometimes it helps to jot down what you are thinking on a piece of paper and draw it on an oval that represents an ice rink.

So far, we can see that a body or tracing design is like a word. Several of these designs together become a phrase pattern. Two or more phrase patterns become a phrase group.

Exercises for phrase groups

1. Try to identify the musical phrases in a program. A musical phrase is a short musical passage forming a more or less independent member of a group.
2. Create at least three of your own phrase groups of several different but related phrase patterns, identifying and expressing the phrase patterns in the music.

Sections

Sections are made up of several, sometimes many phrase groups in the slow and fast parts of a program. If you create a program consisting of a fast, slow and fast part, you will have three sections in your program. It is well to think of each section being a cohesive one with a theme or motivation. There can be an overall theme, and each section could have a different motivation. As you choreograph, analyze your program:

1. How many sections?
2. How many phrase groups in each section?
3. How many phrase patterns in each group?
4. Are the phrase patterns related to the phrase groups?
5. Are the phrase groups related to the sections?

Design in Time

Movement designs are also accomplished through the passage of time. A specific amount of time passes as your program develops. As one phrase pattern follows another, turning into a phrase group, perhaps 20 seconds have gone by. As one phrase group follows another, perhaps another 30 or 40 seconds goes by. The passage of time establishes a total design encompassing the body and tracing designs, as well as the design on the ice surface. Therefore, a phrase group is also a design in time because time has passed in performing all the designs in space that have become phrase patterns and then phrase groups.

It is possible to create body designs that are wonderful in space but when connecting the designs together to form a phrase pattern, it may not be a satisfactory design in time. The problem may be in the transitions. They may not fit the music, or they may be completely unrelated to each other. The same applies to phrase groups. Each phrase pattern may be satisfactory in time, but when connected with another phrase pattern may not be a good design in time. It is like fitting pieces of a mosaic together. Each piece in itself may be beautiful but it must also fit with the pieces around it to form a complete, beautiful picture. The entire skating program when completed should be a composition made up of smaller patterns that all fit together. Design in time is done through phrase development, which includes the expenditure of energy at various rates, followed by rests. There should be a recognizable shape from beginning to end with differences in length for variety, incorporating dynamics, qualities, rhythm, and elements of movement. Emotional motivation will affect different parts of the body, and how they look in space, so that should be considered also.

It is important that you consider the overall shape of your movement sequences as to structure, content, and form. If one movement grows out of the other, and makes possible the next movement, that is a good design in time. You can get used to thinking this way as you choreograph. You can imagine the designs in your head and how they will connect with each other to make phrase patterns, phrase groups, and what the relationship in time is to the whole piece.

It is rewarding to try consciously to choreograph in time, constructing phrase patterns. As your work progresses, it becomes easier and you will find phrase patterns will form with less effort. This also applies to the ice surface design. It is beneficial to draw your skating patterns on paper and see how the designs fit together. Unusual ice patterns can be invented in this manner.

Exercise for design in time

1. Select a theme or motivation for each section of the music.
2. Design phrase patterns into phrase groups for each section.
3. Go over everything to make sure the design in time is satisfactory.
4. Try choreographing the beginning and ending before you start, based on your motivational theme.

If you find after working hard on your design in time it is still unsatisfactory, it may be that the transitions need to be changed so that they blend better. The transitions between patterns are of the utmost importance. How you establish the design in time controls the artistry of the composition of the skating program. How the skater performs it is the artistry of the style.

Design on the Ice Surface

It is important to establish a good design on the rink surface. You don't want your program to go around in circles. When drawing a design on paper, incorporate as many geometric shapes as you can. Then mark in the elements before beginning to choreograph. You have the ability to change the shape of the design to make it an interesting one, and one that uses the entire surface. After working this way for a time you will find that you will be able to design the program without needing to draw it out.

> *Form and space are one and the same after all, and so are the problems they pose. You can truly understand the shape of something if you know what it is like from all around. You must come to realize what volume, what shape would be displaced if you took that form away, leaving only emptiness in its place.*
>
> —Henry Moore

-9-

Music

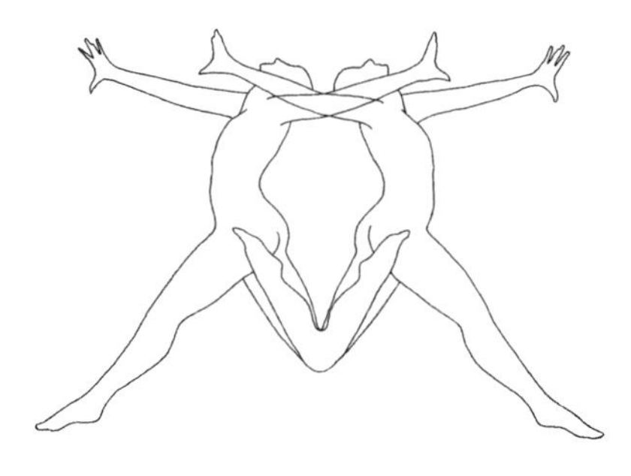

You do not need to be a musician to be a choreographer for skaters, although understanding the basics of written music will help you to explore new relationships between movement and music. In my first book *Choreography and Style for Ice Skaters,* Chapter 2, you can learn some music basics that will help you to count and to better understand your selected music.

Today most tapes and CDs that a choreographer works with are "cuts" from various kinds of music. You do not have the opportunity of a written score (sheet music) to look at and identify the structure of the music. You will have to listen to the music repeatedly to find out where all the dynamics and qualities are.

Note values

It is helpful to your choreography to be able to identify measures of music (sometimes referred to as *bars*) that could transfer into a phrase pattern; and with following measures into a phrase group. By doing that you will be able to build the structure so it can be more easily choreographed.

Fig. 9.1 A music staff divided into measures

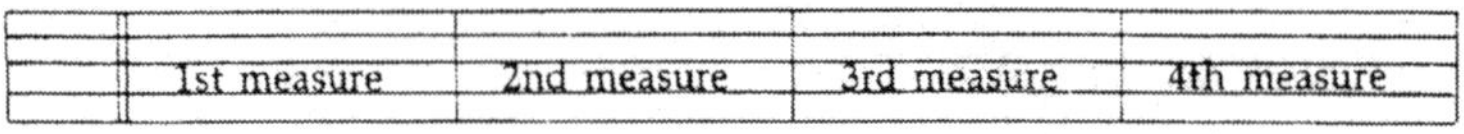

1st measure | 2nd measure | 3rd measure | 4th measure

Many times a basic beat, or count, is represented by a quarter note. This affects all other notes. (See Fig. 9.2.)

Fig. 9.2 Musical notes show how long to hold a sound

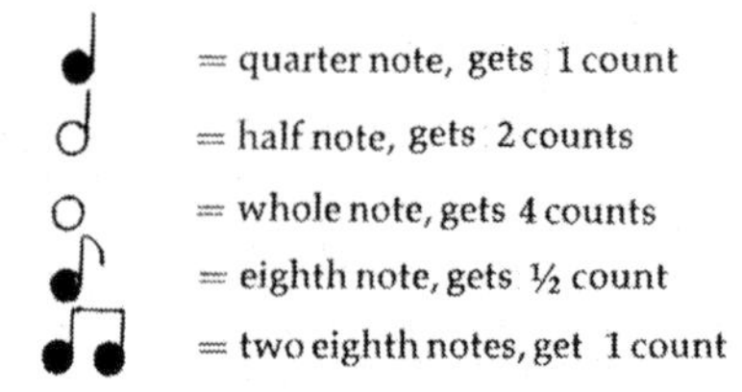

Listen to the music repeatedly to identify the time signature. Two numbers make up the time signature. (See Fig. 9.3) The top number is the *meter*, and indicates how many counts are in a measure. The bottom number signifies what note gets one count. If it is 4/4, that means there are four counts in a measure and the quarter note gets one count. If it is 4/2 then the half note gets one count. If it is 4/8 it means the eighth note gets one count. The quarter note, the value of one count, is the most common, therefore let us be concerned with only the 4/4 and the 3/4 time signatures.

Fig. 9.3 Identify the time signatures

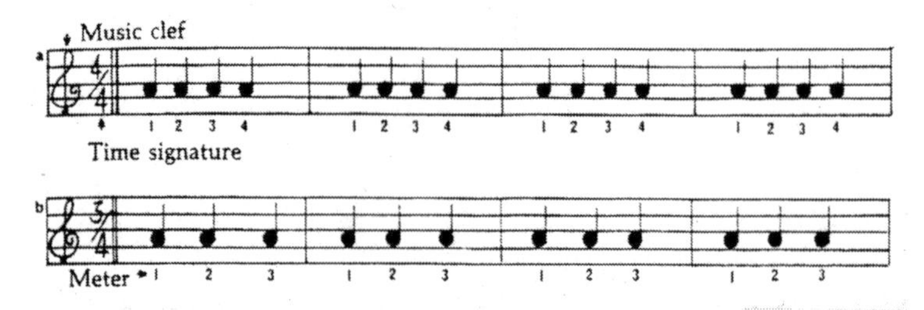

You have to be able to recognize the accents or stresses in the music to recognize the meter. Breaking up the meter into different note values produces rhythm, but each measure must still contain the proper amount of counts. (See Fig. 9.4) Rhythm is time cut up. Of all the elements in skating, rhythm is the most compelling, convincing, and impressive. Yet, much of the time it is the least emphasized. Rhythm produces different types of music like the Tango, Waltz, Foxtrot, Rhumba, Rock and Roll, Bolero, etc.

Fig. 9.4 Division of meter is rhythm

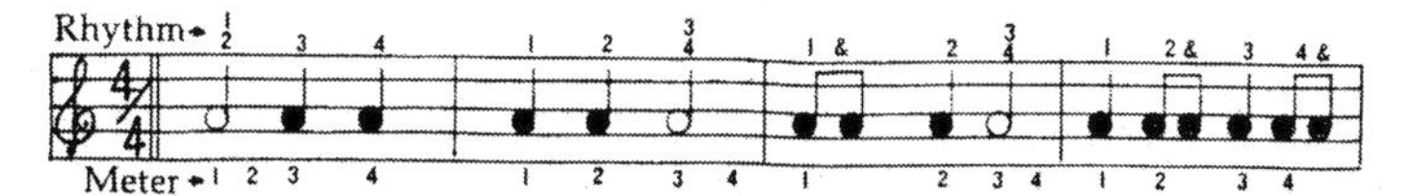

To help you identify each measure, listen for the accents in the music. An accent is a note that is stressed, making it louder than the others around it. Listen to how often the accent occurs. If the stress is on every fourth count then the music is in 4/2, 4/4, or 4/8 time, (four counts to a measure). If the stress is on every third count then the music would be in 3/2, 3/4, or 3/8 time (three counts to a measure). If the stress is on every other count, then the music is in 2/2, 2/4 or 2/8 time. Of course there are more complicated time signatures that need not be discussed at this time. In Fig. 9.5 the strong accents are marked with >. You can also mark them with _.

Fig. 9.5 Stresses help identify the measure

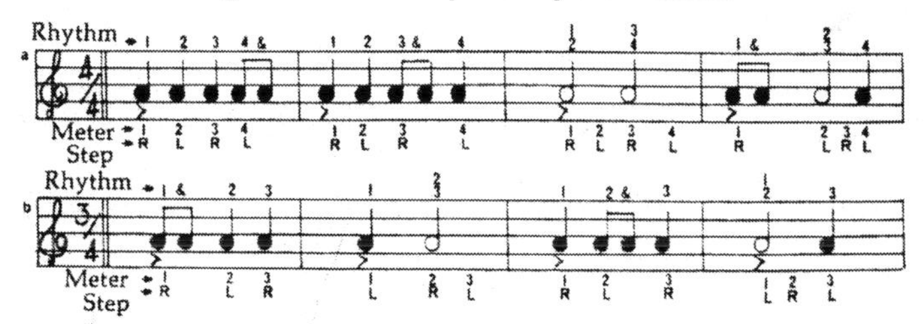

It will help you to know the following four types of 3/4 rhythms:

1. Waltz—has an even rhythm; the counts are evenly distributed.
2. Mazurka—has the accent on the second count.
3. Polonaise—has the accent on the first count.
4. Bolero—is played in triples (three notes are played in the time of one count).

The Polka and the Tango are both in 2/4 time, but the Tango has the stress on the second count, while the Polka has the stress on the first count.

The more you listen to the music, the more you will discover something new each time. You also will be able to get an approximate count of the music. Record the counts on paper in measures, by paying attention to the stresses. You can underline each count that signifies the stress, e.g.:

1234 123 123 12 12

Match your movement phrases and groups to the music measures you have written.

Syncopation

Sometimes the music is very difficult to count. If after repeated listening you still cannot count it, just ignore it, and work to your own counts, which can result in a *syncopated* rhythm. This can be very exciting, especially in footwork. Syncopation is ignoring the normal accent or stress by putting emphasis on a weak beat rather than a strong one, or by an accent falling between the beats. Another way to say it is: *syncopation is a deliberately misplaced accent.*

Listen for the stresses in the music and record them in your own manner. You can put stresses in unexpected places and eliminate moving to some counts. This will produce a syncopated rhythm. If you do nothing on the count following the accented one, it will be more effective.

Here is an example: (See Fig. 9.6)

-	is normal
x	is a heavy stress
o	ignores the note

Fig. 9.6 Syncopating Rhythm

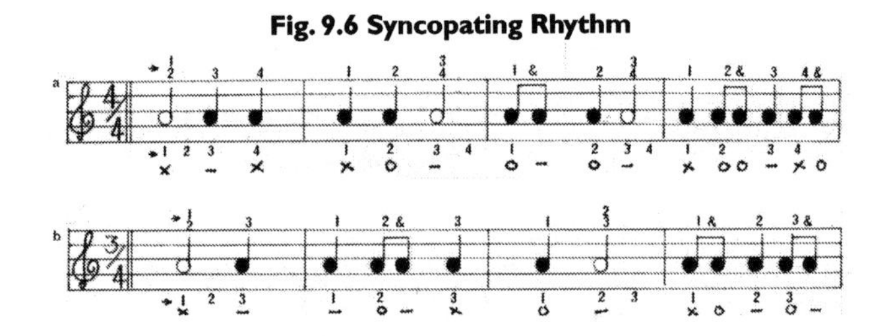

Exercises in syncopation

Before beginning the following exercises, go back to Figures 9.4, 9.5, and 9.6 and clap the rhythm to each measure. Repeat this until you can clap the rhythm without stopping after each measure.

1. Draw a staff in 4/4 time with 4 measures.
2. Put in quarter, half, and eighth notes.
3. Using the key above, mark at random under each note: -, x, or o.
4. Clap out the rhythm you have created.
5. Experiment with footwork to that rhythm.
6. Repeat all of the above in 3/4 time.

7. Experiment with torso and arm movements to that rhythm.

Choreographic repetitions

Motivation provides the energy, endurance, resiliency, and sense of humor that keeps you going. It is that inner drive or impulse that causes a person to do something. It can make you improvise for hours on some image, and throw out endless amounts of material because they are not exactly right. It is your clarity of intention that helps you to determine which material fits and which can be thrown out.

But in skating, often paid by the minute, choreographers are not given that luxury. So intuition and experience will cause you to make quick, sometimes repetitive choices that you know will work. Repetition works out well in dance because of the lengthy time element, and choreographic repetitions are used frequently throughout a work. Repetitions are used to bring out a certain emotion or aspect of the piece. This works well, as usually the dance lasts anywhere from 10 to 45 minutes. Many times they coordinate with repetitions in the music. If used too frequently in skating programs repetitions may be tedious. However, there is a way to use this idea that will result in interesting patterns.

Exercises for choreographic repetitions

1. Create several movements into a phrase pattern
2. Create four phrase patterns.
3. Name each phrase pattern you have created with an alphabet letter. e.g.:

a. Phrase Pattern	A
b. Phrase Pattern	B
c. Phrase Pattern	C
d. Phrase Pattern	D

4. These four phrase patterns have now become a phrase group, with transitions suitably placed to bring it all together cohesively. Now you can experiment by making different combinations.
5. Write down as many combinations you can think of involving these four letters, e.g.:

ABCD	CDBA	ACBD
DCBA	BCDA	ABDC
BACD	ADCB	DABC
CBAD	ADBC	etc.

6. Combine the phrase patterns to match any of these and you have a completely new choreographic movement, or phrase group, based on your original movements.

Pay close attention to the transitions in each phrase group. You can now experiment with these phrase groups in different sections of your program, using various dynamics and qualities. It's fun to experiment with movement this way, as they are all related to each other. You get very interesting effects without looking like literal repetitions.

IMPORTANT: Be sure you are reflecting the musical phrases when creating the phrase patterns, so that you are interpreting the music.

Variations on a theme

Any music that can be carried out in movement can be used in choreographing a theme. You can use ballet, modern, jazz, ethnic (reflecting a nation—although composers today are more international); electronic (produced by electronic instruments or computers), and *music concrete* (made up of sounds of actual things, sometimes distorted).

As has been discussed, learning to read notes and their time values adds much to your skills in interpreting and expressing music, as well as being able to count the music properly to prepare you for the choreographic experience. Many times the composer uses variations on a basic theme. A *theme* is like a song. It is usually more than eight bars, and has two or three sections to it. A *variation* is a modification of the rhythm, harmony, melodic pattern, etc. of a basic idea or theme, usually as a part of a series of such changes but always retaining its identity. In other words, the melody is always there, but changes occur rhythmically by using certain mechanical processes. *Theme and variation* is a form in which a musical idea is stated and then repeated with various modifications.

If your music is cut to include a variation on the theme, you might consider doing a variation of the movement you originally choreographed. You can do this by becoming aware of inventions in music. An invention is a type of short composition based on one or more simple themes, pertaining to counterpoint. In an invention you will hear the melody stated, then sometimes repeated, but not as a whole. You will hear fragments of the stated theme. The composer will take one melody and digress, perhaps transposing it to another key, as well as other variations.

For choreographic purposes, by understanding even a few of the mechanics in variations, you can become more adept in creating movements that express music. Although there are more, I have chosen four inventions that work well with skating programs.

Elision

This means to leave some notes out of the basic theme. It is like saying "can't" instead of cannot, or "don't" instead of do not. It is very easy to see how you can apply this to movement. At the points of omission in the musical phrase, you can omit that part of the movement you originally set. However, you must take care to see that there is a suitable transition connecting the movements together.

Augmentation

The composer takes notes from the basic theme and augments the note values so they have a greater value than those first used. If there were two quarter notes having one count each in the theme, they might become two half notes, each having the value of two counts. Here again, you could use your theme movements and hold them for a longer period of time.

Diminution

This is the opposite of augmentation. It is the restatement of a theme or thematic pattern by shifting the rhythm; placing the bar line differently. The whole or parts of a phrase are squeezed together because the note values are shorter. A half note (two counts) could be changed to a quarter note (one count). You can then take these shorter time values and match them up with the movements in that same part, but decrease the time these movements are held.

Inversion

One way to invert is to change the position of the notes to upside down. The first note remains the same. If the notes go up so many places, then in inversion, they go down so many places. They can be reversed or played backwards.

Inversions need not be constant and can be recognized by rhythm and melodic patterns. This becomes a very interesting way to choreograph. You can take a small section and invert the moves so that the last move becomes the first one, and the first move then becomes the last. Here again, you must make the changes necessary to blend the movements into each other. It will result in an entirely different look.

It is interesting to take a musical score and look for the variations on the theme. You can learn to see the variations more clearly and quicker than by listening to the music. Whether you follow a score, or find the variations by listening to the music; using the idea of changing movements by following the variations of elision, augmentation, diminution and inversion can open up ways of creating new movement ideas.

Selecting music

Select music that can be interpreted rather than used as a background for skating feats. Look for the dynamics and qualities and how the music is phrased for an element of surprise and drama. If the music stirs up a strong emotional feeling, you will have a better chance of interpreting it into movement with expression and feeling.

In making the transitions from fast to slow or slow to fast, there should always be consideration given to the blending of the last note of the first part and the first note of the following part. Even if you end one part with a stop, try to find music that starts on the same note, or has a complimentary note to the music just used. It could be the same note an octave higher or lower or one that is within the harmonic interval of a related chord.

If the music at the end of your program has a dull ending, it is perfectly all right to find an "ending" in an entirely different piece of music. This might mean a phrase of several measures, several notes, or perhaps only one existing note.

Always be aware of who will be skating to this music. If your skater needs strengthening, very strong music may make the skater look weak. Forte exercises practiced during the year can improve that condition.

Making your own musical score

I have always enjoyed choreographing from a musical score, where all the qualities, dynamics, and other musical directions are laid out in front of me. If you can read music, this is a most wonderful way to choreograph. Once you have listened to the music and have a general idea of the style of the movement you wish to use, then put the music away and just read the score. You will find many instructions in the score that, if applied correctly, will enhance the artistry of the choreography. Once you have designed a small part to the score, then try it with the music, and you will be truly amazed at how well it fits. You will hear the subtleties in the music that you did not hear before.

If you have not had the opportunity to learn how to read music, you can make a personal music score. Make a "key" first of symbols, partly in counts and partly with patterns made up of different-sized marks and signs to signify various changes in the music. After listening to the same passage over and over, trying to get every sound that was in the tape, start recording it little by little. (See Fig. 9.7) Make it simple enough so that you can remember the sounds and be able to mark them down as you listen to the music. The symbols can be various sizes to differentiate between loud and soft sounds and low and high sounds. Anything will work as long as you understand your key.

Fig. 9.7 Key for a Personal Score

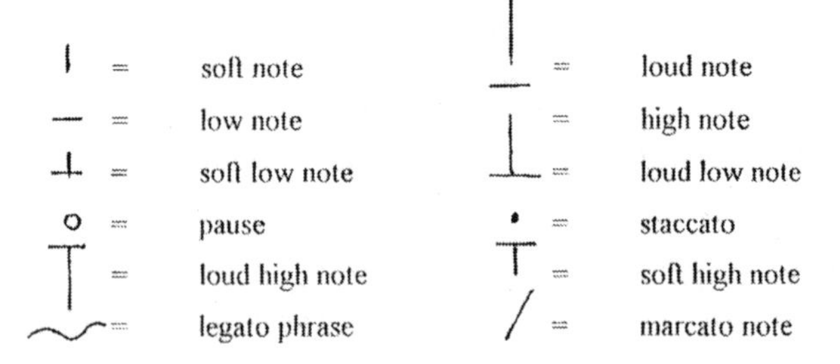

Every program you choreograph will have different music, so you will find yourself adding and subtracting certain symbols to your key. Keeping these personal music scores will eventually enlarge your vocabulary. (See Fig. 9.8)

Fig. 9.8 A Personal Score

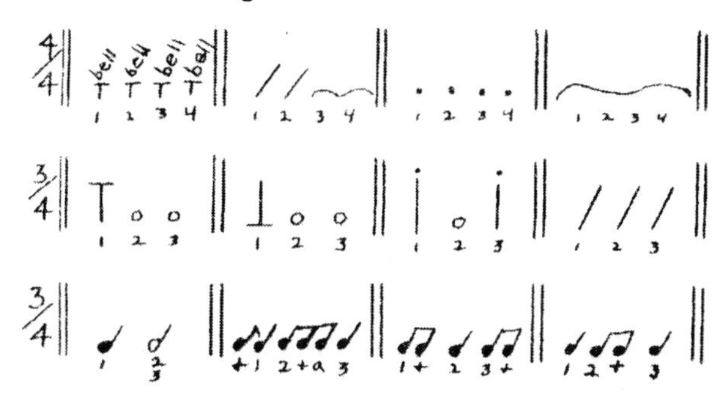

After all the passages are recorded, the choreographic process begins. Make an outline specifying certain phrases of movement, each fitting a certain length of music and each conveying through movement a certain phase of action.

Exercise for choreographing from your personal score

When you have completed your score, begin choreographing movement. First, listen to a brief passage on the tape, checking the score to be sure you recorded it accurately. After playing it two or three times, shut the music off. When you create a movement, work only from your notes. In this way you will be able to concentrate on patterns and movements without the distraction of the musical tempo, which is the relative speed at which a composition is rendered.

Of course, motivation comes first and determines the gesture needed, and the attitude of the movement. Devise the gesture to make the motivation clear. Extend and abstract the gesture into a movement that you feel is strong enough to have an emotional impact on the audience. Then put the music on and make adjustments wherever necessary. You will be pleased to find that this method will stimulate the creation of new and unique movements.

Think of music as form moving in sounds. You want the program to look like the music. As you explore new relationships between music and movement, you will be achieving new choreographic endeavors.

-10-

Gesture

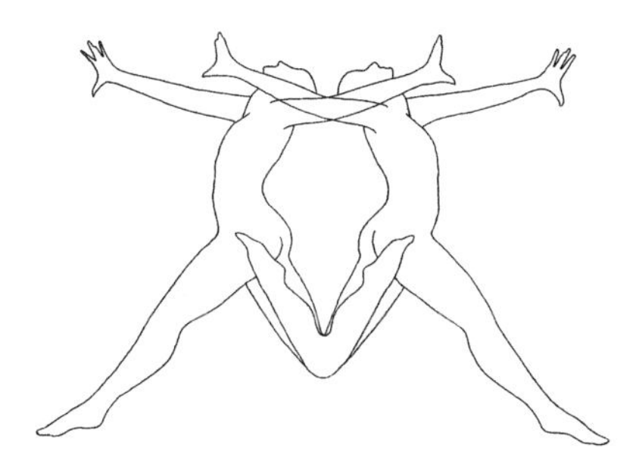

A gesture is a learned patterned behavior. It has movement symbols of one or several parts of the body, which illustrate the drama of a thought. Gesture provides an outline for layer upon layer of interpretive meaning in a program distinctly your own. You can help skaters at all levels add unique character, beauty and imagination to their performances by incorporating gesture.

Many gestures are recognizable anywhere in the world. These behavioral patterns have been learned from infancy by exposure to cultural customs, through friendships and family environment. Most can be understood without words, e.g.:

1. Gently squeezing a loved one's hand.
2. Waving hello or goodbye.
3. Stamping your foot in anger.
4. Lowering your eyes when embarrassed.

5. Tilting your head to the side in uncertainty.
6. Pacing the floor in impatience.

Motivation is the thinking process before a gesture is made. It is a thought that gives the reason for moving in a particular way: For example: A skater has just been given a 6.0. and is so full of joy, she hugs her coach. Hugging is a literal gesture. When a gesture exactly represents what you are thinking or saying, it is called a literal gesture, e.g.:

7. Point to the moon and say "Look at the moon."
8. Beckon with your hand and pat a chair for "Come sit down."
9. Shake your head "No."

Literal gestures that are common in drama have almost no place in skating programs. Gestures can be divided into four categories. The following are some examples:

Social Gesture...incorporating

Waving	Curtsey	Handshake
Bowing	Kissing	Embracing
Smiling	Beckoning	Nodding
Saluting	Farewell	Hugging

Antisocial Gesture...incorporating

Hitting	Slapping	Repelling
Shoving	Stamping	Frowning
Fighting	Shaking fists	Thumbing nose

Emotional Gesture...incorporating

Love	Hate	Fear
Sadness	Excitement	Embarrassment
Happiness	Worry	Confusion
Anger	Despair	Grief

Functional Gesture...incorporating

Gathering	Reaching	Listening
Rocking	Combing	Throwing
Gripping	Picking	Poking
Shoveling	Carrying	Ironing
Washing	Brushing	Sweeping

The gestures above can all be used in drama. But for skating and dance, you want to turn them into abstractions. Using choreography with literal interpretation minimizes the beauty of its form. First take one of the literal gestures and extend it. Extending a gesture is expanding it, stretching it out in every way. It becomes a literal gesture exaggerated.

Gestures in space are filled with expressive interpretations. Taking the literal gesture and extending changes the quality. You can begin to see glimpses of usable dance or skating movements. Taking the extension and abstracting it, produces an artistic movement that can be used repeatedly.

To abstract a gesture or activity is to find a different way, perhaps using a different part of the body, to do the movement, while maintaining the same motivating thought. This encourages you to use your limbs, head and torso in ways you might not have thought of if you had not been trying to express a thought in abstraction.

You have to abstract from something. In my opinion there is no such thing as an abstract movement in itself, even if it is something as simple as a line or a circle movement. Understanding the basic meaning of movement will help you to take a significant, meaningful human gesture and abstract it. The abstraction will develop into movement that is permeated with the original meaning, but is intensified and strengthened and more powerfully conveyed to the spectator.

In skating, it is not important that the abstracted gesture be understood as far as the skater's motivating thought is concerned. It is not necessary for every spectator or judge to feel the same thing. What does matter is that skaters make the audience feel *something* when they are expressing themselves. The most powerful of all gestures are those that affect spectators without their conscious knowledge of why they are being affected.

Many abstractions of gestures develop over time. Bows were abstracted many years ago. It began when someone prostrated himself so that his enemy could see he would not resist. Then there was voluntary prostration caused by fear and cunning. They showed submission to conquerors. Then one day, an enthusiastic slave just dropped to one knee with an upturned face. As civilization advanced, there were heavier and costlier clothes, so there was just a notion of kneeling, which eventually resulted in the artistic bow.

We can say then, that bowing abstracted itself over a period of time.

Preliminary exercises for abstracting gestures

1. Select a functional gesture, e.g.: peeling a banana.

2. Go through the entire process of peeling a banana literally, starting from walking into the kitchen, selecting the banana, peeling it, discarding the peels, and walking out of the kitchen.

3. Be very detailed. Don't leave anything out.
4. Extend the literal function of peeling the banana by exaggerating everything you have done. If you used levels in your literal function, be sure you exaggerate the levels in your extended one.
5. Abstract the extended gesture by asking yourself:
   a. How many different ways can I do this gesture, using different parts of my body but with the same intention?
   b. What other level in space can I use?
6. Pick out several more from the other categories of social, emotional, and anti-social gestures. Do them literally and then extend and abstract them. Taking basic gestures and abstracting them can achieve artistic qualities.

Advanced exercises for abstracting gestures

1. Pick an existing short story, or write an original one.
2. Mark all the literal gestures to be used in the story.
3. Create a choreographic study based on the story.
4. Take each gesture and extend it by exaggerating it fully.
5. Take each *extended* gesture and abstract it.
6. Fit transitions into your choreographic study.

Gestures of the Hands

Gestures in which the hand touches the head or the face can have deep implications and expressive value. It depends on where the hand is placed. If you intend to indicate strong physical meaning or passion, the hand on the back of the head would be appropriate. The hand near the top of the head would indicate a mystical or reverent quality. The hand touching or near the forehead indicates thought or meditation. If you want to give the feeling of tenderness or affection, use the hands around the upper cheeks. The lower cheeks would indicate a more sensual feeling.

At one time it was the fashion in skating to keep the arms outstretched with the palms up. I always objected to this as it seemed all expression was lost; no matter what the skater was doing, the hand position never changed. The position of the hands and palms all have special meaning, and even though the audience might not know exactly what the expression is that is being represented, the basic meaning is conveyed. It must be remembered that the hand, as well as the face, is part of the body; and the entire body should express the same thing. If the body is free and saying one thing, and the hands are still and tight, the intended expressive purpose is lost. The skater should be able to produce hand gestures that say the same thing that the body is saying.

Shoulder gestures can impart deep meaning into a program. A strong emotion can be expressed by the elevation of a shoulder. When you use an elevation of the shoulder it increases the expression of gestures in other areas. On the other hand, the effect of effortless lightness can be achieved in elevation only if the shoulder is relaxed and not lifted.

Gesture is used in order to indicate and assist what man is trying to say in words. Gesture is the speech of the body. It is very potent, and sometimes remembered more than words. To take a significant human gesture extend and abstract it, repeating it with different rhythmic patterns—making it into skating movement—can increase the eloquence of its power, as long as the abstract movement does not convey an opposite intention.

It is interesting that you can have a basic literary idea generate to the viewer an abstract arrangement of forms. It fuses these forms with a quality that makes them more meaningful to people. Gestures in skating offer the opportunity to express emotions that will be remembered long after the program has been performed.

-11-

Movement as it Relates to Space

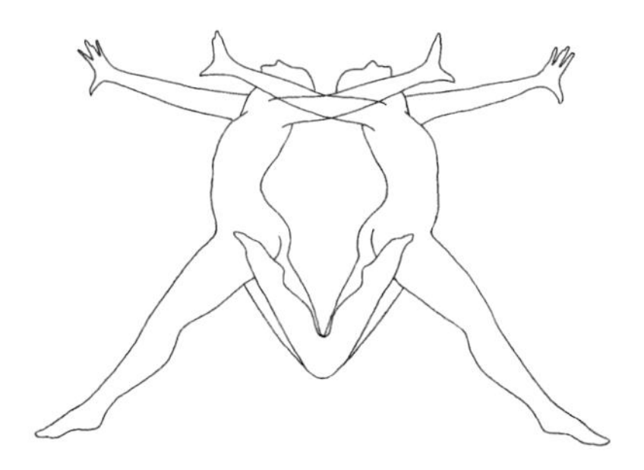

Martha Graham, Charles Weidman, and Doris Humphrey were the three pioneers of modern dance in our country in the early years of the 20th century. Before them, the influences of Isadora Duncan, Ruth St. Denis and Ted Shawn made possible those changes. These wonderful dancer/choreographers, along with the theories of Francois Delsarte, made discoveries of how every movement made by the human body has a design in space and an energy flow. These concepts are still being used today in the dance world, and subsequently have flowed over into the skating world.

Symmetry and Asymmetry

There are certain basic ingredients that can be said to be constant in design. These are the ingredients of symmetry and asymmetry, or balance and imbalance. Symmetry in body positions brings forth the feeling of peace and serenity. *Symmetry occurs when the design is exactly the same on both sides of center.* It suggests stability, strength and authority; and is important for moments of rest and repose. Absolute balance is always good when used at the beginning of a sequence to indicate a certain serenity before high activity has begun. Symmetry is safe but it can be overdone, and you must be careful that the choreography does not result in monotony and boredom. There needs to be contrast in the program both in music and in movement.

Because skating is about moving and dynamism; its moments of excitement and highest interest are usually asymmetrical, with symmetrical forms being used for contrast, points of departure and closing. Skaters can use all the parts of their bodies in many combinations and in all directions. They can include dynamics and rhythms to portray conflicting emotions, but they need a balanced design if a rest is required.

Asymmetrical body positions are not just slightly different on both sides, but decidedly so. Even in stillness, asymmetry implies movement and excitement. These movements can be funny or tortuous. They can be filled with variety, contrast, complexity; and they can be risky. Asymmetry is the language of distortion, pain, the grotesque or deformed.

Within the categories of symmetry and asymmetry are two subdivisions:

1. Designs that utilize angled lines.
2. Designs that incorporate curved lines.

Angled lines always suggest force, energy and vitality, emphasized by lines moving in opposite directions. They are good for themes of conflict, and can also reflect joy and hope. Angled lines are the most stimulating.

Curved and straight lines are the most soothing. However, in between the two there is a gradation, with symmetrical designs utilizing angles, and asymmetrical designs utilizing curves and straight lines. Starting with this concept, you can begin to plan a program, deliberately using designs that fit the closest to your choreographic ideas. If your motivation is expressing love (See photo, page 75), movements should be in curved or circular designs. If you want to portray enthusiasm, use quick movements with angled lines.

Symmetrical and asymmetrical shapes are *body* designs. They do not change their shape while skating. They may be held for a moment or longer, but the shape does not change.

Exercises for symmetry and asymmetry

1. Create a short choreographic study using symmetry.
2. Select a motivational theme.
3. Repeat above using asymmetry.

(In all the exercises use as much as you can from previous chapters.)

Symmetry

Asymmetry

Successions

Successions are movements passing through the entire body, or any part of the body, which moves each muscle, bone and joint as it comes to it. Think back to the single energy ball exercises. Those are successive movements. They are wave-like movements. Successive movements are the most important for expressing emotional qualities.

There are two major kinds of successive movements:

Love

1. True successions
   a. Movement begins in the center of the body and works outward.
   b. These kinds of movements represent beautiful and loving emotions
2. Reverse successions
   a. The movement begins in the extremities and works inward to center.

b. These kinds of movements represent insincerity, falseness and evil qualities.

Exercises for successions

1. Compose a choreographic study using true successions, and portraying love.
2. Compose a study using reverse successions, and portraying evil.
3. Compose a study using true successions and symmetry.
4. Compose a study using reverse successions and asymmetry.

Oppositions and Parallelisms

Oppositions are moving designs (*tracing* designs). They are any two parts of the body *moving* in opposite directions simultaneously. Oppositions relate feelings of strength, force, and emotional or physical power. When oppositions are used with successions, it adds strength to the successions. Compare oppositions with asymmetry. Asymmetry is a body design; it *does not move.* No expression of strength is possible unless somewhere in the body an opposition is taking place.

When you use oppositions with successions, it adds power to the purpose for which successions are being used. A simple rejecting movement of the hand and arm, without any movement in the body elsewhere, would be weak. But, add to the movement of the hand and arm, a strong opposed movement of the head and upper torso, and you produce a stronger expression.

The skating body should work in oppositions:

1. As the knee bends (plié), the torso should stretch up.
2. Think of the camel spin as a three-way stretch: extended leg, body and arms.
3. In a camel spin with a plié, free leg stretches out as the knee bends.

Oppositions are good for what I call *corrective choreography.* Skaters sometimes have difficulty in learning a layback because one shoulder is held lower than the other. Instead of directing them to raise that shoulder, ask them to lower the opposite one.

Exercises for oppositions

Prepare choreographic studies using:

1. Oppositions with asymmetry.
2. Oppositions with true successions.
3. Oppositions with symmetry.

4. Oppositions with reverse successions.

Parallelisms

Parallelisms are two parts of the body *moving* in the same direction at the same time. Compare parallelisms with symmetry. Symmetry does not *move*; it is a body design. Parallelisms are tracing designs as they are *moving*. They have a tendency to look weak, but can be used for design, decorative and stylized movement.

Exercises for parallelisms

Prepare choreographic studies using:

1. Parallelisms with symmetry.
2. Parallelisms with oppositions.
3. Parallelisms with asymmetry.
4. Parallelisms with successions.

Fear

Emotions

There is a psychological division of space that surrounds the skater's body that can be divided into three parts.

1. In the front
   a. Things seem best; better known, better understood and feared less. Things are more vital.
2. At the sides
   a. The sides suggest more magnitude and are more emotional.
3. Behind
   a. Projects fear (see photo, above), negative feelings, rejection.

Graphing in space, emotionally and with feeling, goes beyond normal or natural. Otherwise it is acting, not skating. Emotions are unique to each person, and they will be expressed differently. However, there are certain basic changes the body goes through when an emotion is shown, that will help in determining expressive movement.

Certain gestures are made consciously or unconsciously during pleasure or stress. The following are some changes a body can go through while expressing a particular emotion:

Pride and Arrogance

Joy and Happiness

Anger

1. **Excitement**
   Laugh, smile, eyes look around, jump up and down, hand on mouth, very lively, clasping yourself, clapping, spinning around, explosive movements.

2. **Despair**
   Contractions, hunched shoulders, slow movements.

3. **Pride and Arrogrance**
   Elbows away from the body.

4. **Joy and Happiness**
   Shoulders move up and down, smile, jump up and down, laugh, big eyes, throwing head back, expansive movements, spinning around, successive movements, elevated movements.

Rage

5. **Worry**

   Troubled eyes, become quiet, wrinkle eyebrows, lower lip hangs down, wring hands, pace.

6. **Shame**

   Look down, look unsure, wring hands, withdraw, wriggle, squirm.

7. **Love**

   Smile, curved movements, hold yourself, look dreamy, fluid moves, hands touching mid-torso and upper cheeks, forward leaning movements.

8. **Guilt**

   Hang head down, hands in pocket; look depressed, tense, move with agitation.

9. **Cruelty**

   Stiffens, very upright, towering, harrowed eyes.

10. **Confusion**

    Shrug shoulders, tilt head.

11. **Anger**

    Stamp feet, narrow eyes, glare.

12. **Rage**

    Trembling, clenched fists, tenseness.

Sadness

Hate

Tender or Affectionate

13. Blushing

Turning head away, lowering head.

14. Awareness

Eyes wide, body alert, shoulders back, quickness of movement.

15. Enthusiasm

Elevated shoulders, quick movements, hopping, jumping, clapping hands.

16. Yearning

Reaching out, open palms, leaning forward.

17. Grief

Downward moves, concave arms clasped around torso, forward and back rocking motion of the body, breathing distortions.

Worry, Rejection, Affection, Joy

18. Oppression

Elbows held within the confines of the body.

19. Sadness

Heavy and downward movements, rocking, drooping, distortions, shoulders curved forward

20. Jealousy

Glaring; hands on hips; turning away.

21. Hate

Glaring; fists, arms back.

22. Tender or Affectionate

Hands near cheeks.

There are many more. When observing people experiencing emotional ups or downs, make mental notes of what they do physically. Use these notes to abstract movements that you may be able to use to carry out a motivation in your choreography.

Exercises in choreographing emotions

1. Create a choreographic study, using at least three emotions.
2. Select and tape some music.
3. Write a story surrounding the emotions to fit the music.

4. List the qualities, dynamics, and elements of movement you can use.
5. Select the jumps and spins you want in the program.
6. Draw a rink surface plan, and place the jumps and spins in it.
7. Design the program.
8. Insert symmetry, asymmetry, successions, parallelisms, and oppositions wherever applicable.

Over a period of time, go through the whole list of emotions incorporating them into choreographic studies. You will find you are developing a relationship between yourself and space.

-12-

Image of Yourself as a Choreographer

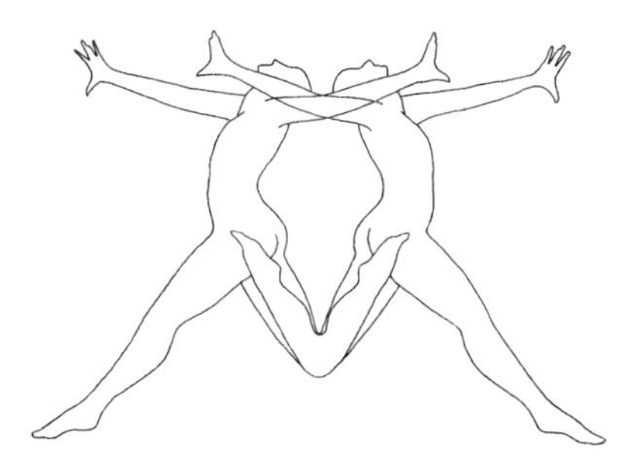

Many coaches stop far short of ever realizing their potential because they feel they don't fit the image of what a choreographer should be. Sometimes they work hard to follow an ideal form that may not suit their bodies. Instead, they should use their natural resources to discover the artist lying dormant within.

What makes you a good choreographer is *not* trying to be someone you're not. You don't become good by wishing you could dance well, had more experience, or were a better skater. What makes a good choreographer is truly being yourself, and creating and moving in your own unique way, based on knowledge learned.

No two choreographers create alike. There is a distinctive style underneath all that you do and personal characteristics that make you the special person and artist you are. The form of your body and how it makes you move, your sense of timing, your feelings and experiences are the raw materials you have to work with as a choreographer.

However limiting they may sometimes seem, they are your lumps of clay, ready to be sculpted into movement. Success depends to a great extent on how effectively you can make your unique qualities of body and spirit work for you.

The way you feel inside is the basis of your choreographic image, and that in turn contributes greatly to how you feel about yourself. By constantly experimenting—creating choreographic studies on the subjects discussed in this manual—your choreographic image will become clearer. Take risks and stretch the limits of what you can do to make yourself aware of your potential. You have the power to alter and change your image, sometimes for the better, and sometimes for the worse. Changing the mental image of yourself affects your creativity. If you constantly think in negatives you may induce problems that were not there to begin with.

Remember, you learn by making mistakes, so take joy in them and go on. When you practice the exercises in this manual, you will begin to realize that you *can* do this. Your brain will send messages to your body to respond to your ideas.

I am a believer in dreams as a process of creativity. When I first began choreographing, I read an article in the *Los Angeles Times* about dreams, and how you can solve creative problems by dreaming. Of course, as I was just beginning I was very intrigued with this idea. It took almost two weeks of thinking hard about choreographic problems just before going to sleep, before it happened. I woke up suddenly at 4:00 a.m. realizing I had been choreographing in my dream. I quickly arose and wrote it all down as I remembered it. It was the answer I needed, and it worked perfectly. Now whenever I have a choreographic problem, I think hard about it and the different ways it can be solved just before going to sleep. It is exciting to wake up in the morning, and find I have been dreaming choreography. Many times the problems are solved in the dream. I get my pad of paper and jot down the ideas I dreamed, knowing if I did not do that, I would forget within the hour. It does not always work, but when it does, it is exhilarating.

Work on a mental picture of yourself and change it to suit your choreographic pursuits. This will alter the way you move and develop new ideas. These ideas will stimulate the nerves, starting the process of moving the muscles and bones. Ideas excite the nerves into action. If you change your way of thinking about movement, you will automatically change your neuromuscular response.

Don't be afraid to fantasize. It is important to dream of yourself choreographing, as all growth and achievement starts with a longing to reach beyond what we are. You can grow and mature through your fantasies, and your dreams can fuel your efforts and spur you on to greater heights. You may not always succeed in achieving what you dreamed, but in the